the Archery Drill Book

STEVE RUIS | MIKE GERARD

HUMAN KINETICS

Library of Congress Cataloging-in-Publication Data

Names: Ruis, Steve, 1946- author. | Gerard, Mike, 1960- author.
Title: The archery drill book / Steve Ruis, Mike Gerard.
Description: Champaign, IL : Human Kinetics, [2020].
Identifiers: LCCN 2019014974 (print) | LCCN 2019018513 (ebook) | ISBN
  9781492588368 (epub) | ISBN 9781492588351 (PDF) | ISBN 9781492588344
  (print)
Subjects: LCSH: Archery--Training.
Classification: LCC GV1185 (ebook) | LCC GV1185 .R85 2020 (print) | DDC
  799.3/2--dc23
LC record available at https://lccn.loc.gov/2019014974

ISBN: 978-1-4925-8834-4 (print)

The web addresses cited in this text were current as of March 2019, unless otherwise noted.

Acquisitions Editor: Diana Vincer; **Managing Editor:** Karla Walsh; **Copyeditor:** Patricia L. MacDonald; **Proofreader:** Leigh Keylock; **Permissions Manager:** Martha Gullo; **Senior Graphic Designer:** Joe Buck; **Cover Designer:** Keri Evans; **Cover Design Associate:** Susan Rothermel Allen; **Photographs (cover and interior):** Steve Ruis and Mike Gerard; **Photo Production Manager:** Jason Allen; **Senior Art Manager:** Kelly Hendren; **Illustrations:** © Human Kinetics; **Printer:** Versa Press

Human Kinetics books are available at special discounts for bulk purchase. Special editions or book excerpts can also be created to specification. For details, contact the Special Sales Manager at Human Kinetics.

Printed in the United States of America

10 9 8 7 6 5 4 3 2 1

The paper in this book is certified under a sustainable forestry program.

Human Kinetics
P.O. Box 5076
Champaign, IL 61825-5076
Website: www.HumanKinetics.com

In the United States, email info@hkusa.com or call 800-747-4457.

In Canada, email info@hkcanada.com.

In the United Kingdom/Europe, email hk@hkeurope.com.

For information about Human Kinetics' coverage in other areas of the world, please visit our website: **www.HumanKinetics.com**   E7532

Tell us what you think!
Human Kinetics would love to hear what we can do to improve the customer experience. Use this QR code to take our brief survey.

Contents

Drill Finder

Drill	Page Number	Shooting	Nonshooting	Recurve	Traditional	Compound
CHAPTER 2 COMPOUND ESSENTIALS						
2.1 Finding Your Natural Stance	52	◉	◉			◉
2.2 Refining Your Stance	54	◉	◉	◉	◉	◉
2.3 Raising the Bow 2	55	◉		◉	◉	◉
2.4 Bow Arm Setting	56	◉	◉	◉	◉	◉
2.5 Bow Shoulder Setting	57	◉		◉	◉	◉
2.6 Introduction to Release Technique	58		◉			◉
2.7 Finding Your Release Anchor Position	60	◉	◉			◉
2.8 Honing Your Release Technique	62	◉				◉
2.9 Triggerless Release Activation	63	◉				◉
2.10 Wrist Strap Release Activation	64	◉				◉
2.11 Drawing Motion	65	◉	◉	◉	◉	◉
2.12 Drawing Elbow Position	66	◉		◉	◉	◉
2.13 Aiming on Center	67	◉	◉	◉	◉	◉
2.14 Mirror Drill (Compound)	68	◉	◉	◉	◉	◉
2.15 Blank Bale Drill	69	◉				◉
2.16 Blind Bale Drill (Compound)	70	◉				◉
CHAPTER 3 FLAWLESS EXECUTION						
3.1 Scoring With Sights	74	◉		◉	◉	◉
3.2 Shooting Fast and Slow	75	◉		◉	◉	◉
3.3 Aiming	76	◉		◉	◉	◉
3.4 Call the Shot	77	◉	◉	◉	◉	◉
3.5 Checking Your Foot-to-Foot Weight Distribution	78		◉	◉	◉	◉
3.6 Plumbing Your Bow 1	80	◉	◉	◉	◉	
3.7 Plumbing Your Bow 2	81	◉	◉	◉	◉	
3.8 Peep Sight Centering	82	◉	◉			◉
3.9 Facial String Clearance and Anchor Drill	83		◉	◉	◉	◉
3.10 Aiming in the Wind 1	84	◉	◉	◉	◉	◉

(continued)

Drill	Page Number	Shooting	Nonshooting	Recurve	Traditional	Compound
5.7 Building and Managing Arrow Counts	129	●		●	●	●
5.8 Shooting Fast and Slow	130	●		●	●	●
5.9 The 1,000-Arrow Challenge	131	●		●	●	●
5.10 The Never-Ending End Drill	132	●		●	●	●
5.11 Basic Drawing and Holding (With a Shot Trainer)	133	●		●	●	
5.12 Reversals With an Elbow Sling Trainer	134		●	●	●	●
CHAPTER 6 CONSISTENCY						
6.1 Bridging	136	●		●	●	●
6.2 Shooting for Groups	140	●		●	●	●
6.3 Checking Your Group Sizes	142	●		●	●	●
6.4 Varying Practice Locations	144	●		●	●	●
CHAPTER 7 BALANCE AND STILLNESS						
7.1 Shooting From Uneven Footing	146	●		●	●	●
7.2 Shooting Off a Balance Board	147	●		●	●	●
7.3 Shooting Off of One Foot	148	●		●	●	●
7.4 Head Rotation and Neck Stretching	149		●	●	●	●
7.5 Head Canting	150	●	●	●	●	●
7.6 Exploring Breathing Patterns	151	●	●	●	●	●
CHAPTER 8 TRAINING MIND-SET						
8.1 Joint and Muscle Activation	154		●	●	●	●
8.2 Flexibility Maintenance	155		●	●	●	●
8.3 Stretch Band Drill	156		●	●	●	●
8.4 Instilling a Shot Sequence	157	●	●	●	●	●
8.5 Building a Mental Game	158	●		●	●	●
8.6 Emphasizing Shot Execution 1	159	●		●	●	●
8.7 Emphasizing Shot Execution 2	160	●		●	●	●
8.8 Imagery Drill	161	●	●	●	●	●
8.9 Fun Visualization	163		●	●	●	●
8.10 Verbal Cuing	164	●		●	●	●
8.11 Staying in the Now	165	●	●	●	●	●

(continued)

Preface

This book is the first of its kind, a book of drills designed to help archers and coaches train more effectively. As coaches, we wish this book had been available when we started out in coaching—it would have saved us a lot of time and effort. If you are a serious competitive archer or an archery coach, this book is a resource of training protocols designed just for you. These drills help archers get things done, be they form corrections, skill additions, or technique adjustments—drills are the way expert archers become expert and advance to elite status.

Drills are provided for every level of archer. If you are a beginner and just getting started or an advanced archer trying to get to the next level, there are drills here for you. You can do many of the drills as a beginner and again in the future when you have progressed into an intermediate archer or even an advanced archer. Reversal drills work for beginners and for everyone else all the way up. Of course, advanced to elite-level archers will be holding their bows at full draw for extended periods, something beginners can't match, but by doing some drills at every level, you get to see, and feel, your improvement. For beginners doing reversals, holding a recurve bow at full draw for five seconds in sets of three repetitions may be a daunting task. Elite archers are able to hold for as long as 30 seconds and do sets of 10. This drill increases strength and stamina and is used worldwide.

Since physical training (e.g., in a gym) is an entire book-length work in itself, here the drills focus on using the archery equipment you already have as the basis for the exercises. You may want to augment these drills by either buying or making helpful pieces of equipment (e.g., rope bows, balance boards). Instructions are provided as to how to find or build these simple devices.

To make this book effective, there is a drill finder up front. After you have familiarized yourself with it, you can jump in and find a drill designed for what you want to accomplish. The drills themselves are described concisely so that you can get right into doing them rather than reading about them. Because we cannot tell what you will have read at any point, there is some repetition so you do not miss important safety instructions or fundamental approaches. Each chapter consists of drills on a common theme and has a short introduction addressing what the drills are trying to accomplish. Each drill has straightforward instructions, tips for getting it done, and often variations that can be used to make the drill more effective. To further enhance these drills, we have included some special features in the book such as favorite drills provided by elite archers and coaches. Additionally, although there is information in the introduction regarding how archery drills can be made fun and into games, we give specific suggestions for some drills throughout the book to highlight which types of drills fit into a game format, and we give some quick and easy examples to help you get started.

Archers often find themselves at their practice facilities with nothing to do but shoot arrow after arrow. Sometimes they shoot practice rounds to see how they are scoring. This is not how elite archers train. Just shooting arrows doesn't cut it. Elite archers choose drills to make changes, shore up weak points in form, and learn new skills. Workouts involve spending a fraction of an hour (typically 10 to 15 minutes) on a drill and then shifting to another drill, working on a small set of changes that need to be learned. The drills offer concentrated effort toward a single goal, focusing your body and mind on getting where you want to go.

This is a pragmatic book designed for archers and coaches seeking to get better. Using the drills in this book is a faster path to improvement than what archers normally do during practice time.

Acknowledgments

I had been in contact with Human Kinetics regarding another matter and had been introduced to Diana Vincer, who had taken over that matter from another HK employee. Our business done, I was a little surprised when contacted by Diana asking us to pitch her a book tentatively titled *The Archery Drill Book* to fit in with a whole slew of other HK books of similar title.

I had been taking notes for such a book for over 10 years, a book I believe is greatly needed by both archers and archery coaches, but I was up to my hips in other projects. But this was HK asking, after all, a company that had been really good to us, publishing our first book, *Precision Archery*.

If you aren't aware, putting together a book like this is a lot of work, and, well, help is really welcome. We asked HK whether coauthors were acceptable (of course!), and the first person who came to mind (Mike Gerard, who has probably forgotten more about archery than I have ever known) said, "Yes!"

So if you have an idea for a book you really want to see in print, getting that idea to a gifted acquisitions editor such as Diana Vincer is a good way to see things get done.

Thanks to all the fine folks at Human Kinetics for doing all the hard work necessary to make books available that help athletes and coaches get better!

And as always, I thank my long-term partner, Claudia Stevenson, for being there by my side, a constant support and inspiration.

—*Steve Ruis*

I wish to thank my coauthor, Steve Ruis, for his desire to work with me on this project and for his patience during this crazy time. His influence and inspiration are why this project has come to completion.

My inspiration to write comes from the great writers who helped me get out of my own backyard in my early teens in the early 1970s. I lived in a rural area where archery coaches and quality information were limited. As a result, I joined a JOAD club at the Bow Rack archery shop in San Pablo, California. We were called the Shooting Stars. The shop owner was Mr. Norm Malonee, and his crew of coaches included him, Fred Spradling, and Jerry West. Although I credit these fine people with giving me a start and foundation to work from, it was the writers of the time who moved me to try things I never dreamed of. And since they were not present, I interpreted what they wrote and applied their teachings in my own unique way. These writers were not only my coaches but also my heroes for giving of their expertise freely and with heart, allowing me to develop as a young archer. These writers include Fred Troncoso, Al Henderson, Len Cardinale, and Shig Honda. There were many others, but the writings of these people in particular left an indelible mark on me. It is the writers of the past who have inspired me to give to the archery community in similar spirit—to pay it forward while giving it back. To all the individuals who have given of themselves in the form of writing a book, thank you.

Other key individuals who I am eternally thankful to are

- Mrs. Marge Callahan, college archery coach at Cal State University at Los Angeles;
- Mr. John Williams, friend, writer, coach, talented archer, and remarkable competitor; and
- last but not least, Mr. Ed Eliason, the single biggest positive influence in my archery career.

I could go on and on with all the great friends and competitors I have had the pure joy, adrenaline rush, and inspiration to compete with over the years. I'm truly honored by your friendships.

—Mike Gerard

We would be remiss if we didn't thank our models, archery champions all (pictured, from left to right): Lindsay Weatherspoon, Sebastian Nguyen, Anna Kemp, and Joel Moreno. We also thank the Datus Archery Club of Salt Lake City for hosting our photo shoot.

Key to Symbols

Each drill is accompanied by symbols that, in short, tell you what kind of archer each drill is intended for. Here are the symbols and their explanations:

This is a shooting drill, either at a target or blank bale.

This drill is a nonshooting drill.

This drill is for recurve archers.

This drill is for traditional archers.

This drill is for compound archers.

Shooting drills must be performed in a safe locale, such as an archery range. Nonshooting drills can be done at home or wherever else it is convenient.

Integrating Drills Into Your Archery Practice

Drills can be a very valuable way to achieve basic archery technique, achieve better archery skills, and correct for problems in your technique and skills. They also can be a complete waste of time if done incorrectly, without appropriate focus, or without appropriate intensity.

We advocate for *deliberate practice*. This seems to be the most effective way to learn any kind of physical skill, even some mental ones. Ordinary practice, usually consisting of just repetition, is ineffective in that mere repetition of a task leads to a performance plateau, with no way to break out of that plateau. If practice alone worked, driving to work for 40 years would prepare you to drive in Formula 1 races. Deliberate practice is structured, effortful practice, usually not all that pleasurable, focused on specific performance bottlenecks. It does allow athletes to break through performance plateaus.

A summary of deliberate practice follows:

- *You must get immediate feedback on performance because you should never let a mistake go without correcting it.* This requires a great deal of focus, especially when learning new shot elements or new executions.

- *You must bring a high level of intensity to your training.* You must deliberately push your limits. This is in contrast to both work (where the goal is pacing yourself to achieve a steady performance) and play (where the goal is to have fun).

- *Deliberate practice is intense and exhausting and can be sustained for only a limited time each day.* There are no benefits from practicing for more than four hours a day, and benefits tail off after about two hours a day. Adequate recovery time is essential. Instead of one four-hour session, two two-hour sessions separated by some activity that allows you to rest is superior.

- *A commitment to deliberate practice involves not just you but a support structure as well.* Support comes from spouses, parents, teachers, and facilities, sustained over a long time. Getting competent coaching can greatly accelerate your learning.

If you are interested in learning more about deliberate practice, we recommend the book *Peak: Secrets From the New Science of Expertise* by Robert Pool and Anders Ericsson. Ericsson created the concept and has done much of the research into this topic.

All the conditions of deliberate practice need to be applied to doing drills. Drills also need to be a part of a personal improvement practice plan. If practice is approached haphazardly, progress will be haphazard. Every archery practice session should have intensions for what you want to achieve. You are unlikely to achieve a great deal with a list like this:

1. Try out new release aid.
2. Tune in new arrows.
3. Shoot practice round.

When you try out any new piece of gear, like a release aid, you need to focus on what you expect from it. Is this new release aid something that will equate to higher scores? If so, you need to test it. Once you have spent enough time with it to be comfortable, you need to schedule something like practice rounds, maybe switching between the old and new releases each end, then see which release produces the better scores or the tighter groups. Or if that is too confusing (or difficult, as your anchor position is likely to be different with the two releases), schedule practice rounds with the new and old release aids (several, actually), and then compare scores or group tightness.

The same applies to tuning in new arrows. If these arrows are identical to your old ones, they should perform identically, if set up properly, so check this. If these are completely new arrows to you, perform some sort of competition between the new ones and your old ones. You do not want to switch to using a new arrow only to find out your scores drop because you don't know how to tune them as well as you did the old ones, or worse, they turn out to be not as good as your old ones.

When you shoot a practice round, what are you trying to achieve? Too many archers think that "shooting a practice round" is the same as "practice," which is nowhere near being true. A practice round is a test. You are testing yourself, new gear (a new release, new arrows, something), and you are keeping track of these scores to see if you are getting better, getting worse, or staying the same. You keep records of these scores (with notes because you are not the only factor in achieving a good score) and compare them with your competition scores.

So if you decide to do a drill, think about how to incorporate it into your practice sessions. How will you determine if the drill is working? How will you determine if you are doing the drill correctly? We provide appropriate guidance with each drill, but you need to do a little work to get the most out of any drills you do. That work is easy enough—simply think about your training sessions before you do them.

To take full advantage of the drills in this book, you must be aware of a number of fundamental concepts. We provide short discussions of those here.

EQUIPMENT

Obviously in archery, the equipment plays a vital role in your success. You cannot afford to adopt the attitude of "when I get good, then I will get really good equipment." You need good equipment from the beginning. But realize that you do not need top-of-the-line equipment. You need good equipment. So what is good equipment?

Good equipment gives you good feedback. What you desire is that if an arrow hits a target in a particular place, it is because of something you, as the archer, did, not because of flaws in your equipment. If you have faulty equipment and mistakenly think that poor-scoring arrows are due to something you are doing, you are wasting time, money, and effort. (Imagine trying to work on your form and execution while shooting with a set of variously bent aluminum arrows.) You need equipment that is capable of better scores than you can shoot. Elite archers generally need elite-level, top-of-the-line equipment because they shoot so very well. Beginners can shoot much lesser equipment and are better off doing so (elite equipment requires a great deal of skill to master and without that skill can produce awful results).

If you are on a budget, using equipment that was highly rated some years ago can be a viable option. You will need technical help from a coach, or shop technician, if you take this route and don't possess the skills to make the used equipment safe and functional yourself.

THE LINES OF ARCHERY

Archery seems simple—pull on the string and let go—but if you want to be accurate shot after shot, then it helps to be aware of the forces involved and how your body must align to them to create that level of consistency. We often refer to alignments of various body parts.

Figure I.1 shows some of the lines used for describing such alignments.

Line of sight—Once set cannot be moved

Plumb line—
Archers need
to stand straight

Primary force line—
Elbow can be higher
but not lower

Arrow line—Must
be in plane with
target center

Hip line—Should
either line up with
heels and shoulders
or be midway

Heel line—
Can be used
instead of toe line

Toe line—
Can be misleading
if feet are flared

a

Figure I.1 The lines of archery.

Plumb line—Archer's head must be straight up and down

Shoulder line— Parallel to arrow line for compound; points to center of pressure on grip for recurve

Scapula line

Spine line— Should be flat and plumb

b

THE ROLES OF YOUR CONSCIOUS AND SUBCONSCIOUS MINDS

While expert archers are shooting, they assign certain tasks to their conscious and subconscious (or unconscious) minds. (Here we use the terms *subconscious mind* and *unconscious mind* interchangeably because for archery, there is no useful difference.) Your conscious mind controls the skill sets you are aware of as they are happening. Your subconscious mind controls the mental skills you are unaware of.

In archery, our conscious minds are focused in "the now," on what we are doing and how we are doing it. This is done mostly by carefully observing every step of a shot and not by giving directions. (Try micromanaging your shots, telling yourself what to do and when to do it, and watch your scores plummet!) Every physical aspect of your shot has a mental aspect too; this is essential to your success and will be a large focus for you as you navigate through the drills in the upcoming chapters.

Our subconscious minds monitor all the internal "feels" associated with a shot as well as control all the muscles involved. Learning how to shoot arrows from a bow involves teaching your subconscious mind how to do just that. Shooting arrows is no different from any other manual task, like tying your shoes, riding a bike, or driving a car. When you first were learning these things, you did them consciously and you were slow and clumsy, making a great many mistakes. Once you learned them subconsciously, they became almost effortless, smooth, and much quicker.

Should Drills Be Used by Archers With Physical Disabilities?

All the experts we have consulted indicate that para-archers train in the exact same way as non-para-archers. Once an archer has adaptions available to them so they can shoot effectively, all the drills we offer seem suitable. No special considerations, other than the ones they normally have made, need to be made.

Archers: We believe any of the drills in this book should be available to you and should help you improve your archery. If anyone counseling you indicates that such drills are not appropriate for someone in your situation, we suggest you seek better counsel.

Coaches: If a drill needs to be adapted for an archer with a physical disability, adapt it. That's why they call it *adaptive archery*!

In chapter 8, Training Mind-Set, we provide drills to help with these tasks, but much of this happens naturally. The emphasis on deliberate practice is key, because if you eliminate mistakes, what you learn will be of high quality and last a long time. If you learn to shoot while incorporating mistakes (often called *form flaws*), you will have to correct those procedures by creating a new correct procedure. The problem is that "how to shoot an arrow from a bow," like "riding a bike," is a program stored in long-term memory. Everything you learn to do that is incorrect is still there in memory and can be called up when you find yourself under competition pressure or feeling intense disappointment. It is best to keep the shelf in your memory labeled "how to shoot an arrow from a bow" as bare as possible. Committing to learning only good ways to do things through deliberate practice is tantamount to this.

COMMON SENSE

If you feel pain during a drill or any part of archery training, stop! You are doing something wrong. Get help. Muscle soreness the day after a strenuous workout is normal, but it should be gone or almost gone the day after that. If the pain persists, get medical help.

KEEP NOTES

When taking archery seriously, there are far too many details to keep them all in your head. Since many very successful archers in the past did it that way, we will not claim you will not be able to achieve expert or even elite status as an archer without taking notes, but why do it the hard way?

When doing drills, you will perform a number of sets containing a number of repetitions of the drill, just like in weight training. Also just like in weight training, you will start with a small number of reps and a small number of sets, then increase both of those over time. If you are doing a half dozen drills, how are you going to keep track of where you are with sets and reps?

Obtain a notebook and take notes. Many people use a calendar to organize their practices. Almost anything will do.

In addition, you need to keep track of your scores, your equipment and equipment changes, and so on. All this can be kept in one notebook.

At the risk of being declared old fuddy-duddies, we do not recommend taking notes on smartphones. Finding such notes can be difficult, plus a number of organizations forbid the use of phones on competition shooting lines. Sometimes paper and pencil is still best; this is one of those times. (There are better uses for your smartphone.)

WORKING OUT

It is an axiom of training that the best exercise is the activity itself. We will show ways to enhance the act of shooting to make it more strenuous for training. If you also want to do physical workouts and you have access to exercise equipment, this is not a bad idea. We recommend getting advice from a qualified sports trainer to design a support program. This is usually a strength development program, but it could include cardiorespiratory exercise too.

TURNING DRILLS INTO GAMES

Drills are repetitious by their very nature and can, therefore, be boring. One way to make practice more interesting is to turn drills into games. We provide examples throughout the chapters of drills that lend themselves well to creating a game situation. These drills are not the only ones that work; in actuality, most drills can be turned into a game using the tips outlined in this section.

The games can be with yourself, in the form of challenges, for example, or with a shooting partner in the form of mini competitions with one another. It is critical to not get lost in the competition and lose focus on doing the drills as correctly as possible.

We urge you to give your imagination free rein to come up with games of your own making. In that spirit, the following is offered as a way to get started, not a complete list by any means.

Note: Trying to cheat a shooting partner in such a contest is considered a major character flaw; don't do this! Not only are you at risk of losing your training partner, but stories will be told and you will be the subject of gossip (not the favorable kind).

Rewards

Practice can be broken up into segments, some of which you will enjoy, others not so much. For the latter, you can tie performance in a drill to a reward. For example, "If I do this drill (three sets of five reps) perfectly, then I can do X. If not, it is a do-over."

You can also have a prize for the winners. For example, create a competition with your shooting partner, and the winner gets a soda from the loser. You can go so far as to have substantial rewards, such as the loser washes the winner's car, but it is best that the rewards be trivial. Some more creative rewards are things like the loser must refer to the winner as "the best archer in the city/county/state/nation/world/solar system/Milky Way/universe (your choice)" until your next joint training session. We recommend that on no occasion should money be involved. A $10 bet may be trivial for one archer but substantial for another.

Basic Structure of Training Games

The purpose of making a drill into a game is just to add a little something that makes the drill more challenging and possibly even fun. For example, reversals (chapter 1) are a strength building drill. Your bow is drawn, you hold for X seconds, and then you let down. That is one rep. Several of those make a set.

To spice it up, you can do reversals with an arrow on your bow and a target in view (start close, very close). After the time for a rep has expired, the shot is loosed and scored. The best score after three sets wins! You can set goals for arrow scores as an additional incentive. This adds depth to the drill because it increases an archer's experience in getting off a clean loose after holding longer than is desirable (in timed rounds, one cannot always let down a shot held overlong). As with the basic drill, maintain intense focus on doing things correctly throughout. *Note:* Start with a very close-up target because the strain of holding can result in erratic looses.

An example when shooting at a common target is to mix up the usual aiming for the center with aiming for an exact score, as in darts. If the scoring goal is 34 points, start shooting for the highest scores you can get (e.g., 5 or 10) until you get close, then aim for a 4 or a 3 to hit the scoring goal. If you go over, your score drops to zero and you have to start again. This has the added benefit of letting you practice "aiming off." It adds competition pressure. You can do this alone as well as against a shooting partner.

Another variation is reverse scoring in which the scoring ring values are inverted (e.g., the 10-ring becomes worth 1 point and the 1-ring worth 10 points, and the 2-ring is worth 9, and so on). You can make up contests for lowest score (aiming for the X-ring and hitting it gets you a zero!) or highest.

Creating Mini Competitions

Start these competitions at shorter distances until you develop skill. If one of you is a better shot than the other, it is traditional to negotiate a handicap, a number of points to be spotted to the weaker shot. It is also traditional to shoot for a prize, maybe a sports drink.

If the training exercise is a practice round, hold a contest for the number of Xs shot, or the number of 10s. If the final score is the subject of the competition, points may be given from the stronger to the weaker scorer. This puts pressure on the stronger archer to shoot better than is ordinary, rather than just better than a weaker opponent.

If the drill is a strength building exercise (such as reversals), it can be handicapped between two opponents by how much resistance is involved or the number of reps per set. If reversals are being done, then each partner can take turns while the other times the reps. The one who can do the most reps, or the longest rep, or the most sets wins.

If competing with yourself, the goal can be to break your record for the most reps, or the longest hold, or anything else you would like to achieve.

Playing these games keeps your mind from wandering while doing drills and practice exercises. Taking turns competing blends rest with drilling well. Handicapping the contests makes sure a stronger shooting partner is challenged as much as a weaker one. Basically, if you can measure some indicator of progress being made, that can be used as the basis for a game.

Chapter 1

Recurve and Longbow Essentials

To learn solid basic technique for shooting your recurve bow or longbow, it is important that you have a clear idea of what kind of shot you are trying to build, so some guidance is necessary. The key to guiding an archer's conscious attention on the shot is a shot sequence, or shot routine. This is a sequence of steps needed to be done to get a high-quality arrow shot. It is beyond the scope of this book to provide a complete treatise on how to shoot, but here is a short introduction to the form that applies to these kinds of bows.

A STEP-BY-STEP APPROACH

The general approach to learning archery technique is to list the steps, also called *form elements*, involved in making a shot. All together, this is called your *shot sequence*, or *shot routine*. Here is an example:

Basic Shot Sequence

1. Take your stance.
2. Nock an arrow.
3. Set your hands.
4. Raise the bow.
5. Draw the string.
6. Find your anchor.
7. Aim.
8. Release the string.
9. Follow through.

With your equipment in hand, following these steps will result in a shot. To make it a good shot, the steps need to be done correctly and in order, and therein lies the task: how to learn a shot sequence so it supports making consistently good shots.

As a famous architect once said, "God is in the details" (not the Devil, as it is commonly misquoted, but God), which means if you want a successful outcome, you need to become comfortable with the details. First you attend to taking your stance; then you stop thinking about your stance and attend to the nocking of an arrow, and so on. Each step may have many substeps. For example, some archers shoot their arrows in a numbered sequence, so they have to select the next arrow as part of step 2 (nock an arrow), along with making sure the index vane is correctly oriented, that the nock snaps onto the string completely (if snap nocks are used), and if a clicker is used, that the clicker is correctly set.

What you are doing at any given moment is the most important part of any shot. But a couple of things are worth emphasizing here. For one, psychologists tell us that in sequences like this one, where each step is basically "set it and forget it," we have about nine seconds in any chain before the first steps start to drift "off." If you think of between steps 3 and 4 as the dividing line between preparing to shoot and the act of shooting, then you have about nine seconds from the beginning of step 4 until the shot is finished if you don't want variations caused by this characteristic we all have.

In addition, just before raising the bow (step 4), many successful archers visualize a complete shot, from their viewpoint and as intensely as they can with sights, sounds, smells, everything. This functions as a set of instructions to the unconscious mind, which is controlling all the muscles involved, and so on, in the plan for this shot. You will have practiced your shot ad nauseam, but which of the many shots practiced is the one needed now? Tell your subconscious mind which plan to follow by doing this visualization.

A shot sequence not only gives archers and coaches a framework for the physical actions of a shot (and terms to describe them) but also provides a framework for the mental program of the archers. The control of an archer's attention is just the beginning of learning about this. If you do not have a shot sequence, you need one, and you need it now. As we said, we do not have the space to go into all of these in great detail, but we can address a few. Let's start at the beginning and then jump to the middle and finally the end: from the alpha to the omega of your shot.

Take Your Stance

The rules of competition vary about where you will stand when you shoot, so consult them for that consideration. (All rules accept standing with one foot on either side of the shooting line, so that is a good place to start.) The details beyond where to stand are many: How far apart need your feet be? What angle should your body make with the target line? How much weight to place on each foot? And all you are trying to do is stand still!

There are consequences to whatever stance you choose. Figure 1.1 shows common stances and foot placement, which can help you determine where you might be most comfortable positioning your feet and your body.

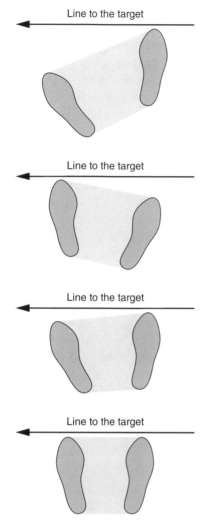

Figure 1.1   Common stances.

Most beginners start with a square, or neutral, stance in which your body faces straight down the shooting line and you are perpendicular to your target. Many advocate for an open stance, in which you turn your body slightly toward the target. Most argue against a closed stance, in which you are turned slightly away from your target. Actually, each stance has strengths and weaknesses. Each can help you address problems with your body alignment while shooting.

For example, the open stance tends to shorten your draw length, so if you are having difficulty overdrawing your bow, it is worth considering. Open stances also make getting into good full draw position more difficult, which is exactly why elite archers favor them. By making good full draw position more difficult to achieve, it makes full draw position more recognizable once you get there (because of the muscle strain needed to adopt it). There is some benefit in twisting your body to get your upper body correctly aligned because that tension makes for a sturdier platform to shoot from.

A closed stance, although out of favor, is out of favor for the wrong reasons. This stance tends to lengthen your draw, and since many beginning archers struggle with getting to full draw, a closed stance can help them do so.

An open stance requires you to turn your head a little less, while a closed stance requires you to turn it a little more. If you are struggling to get your head into position, these are important considerations.

In all cases, a stance's role in a shot is *to support your being still while under the strain of a drawn bow*. That is the criterion to apply when evaluating stances (how still you are at full draw).

Draw the String

All the energy that ends up in the arrow comes from you. By pulling on the bowstring, you change the shape of the bow, and when you release the string, the bow springs back to its original shape, returning the string to its original position and launching the arrow attached to it out into space. The key to doing this over and over the exact same way is to use larger muscles that are more capable of making the draw and not getting fatigued in doing so. This is why most archery technique emphasizes the use of back muscles in the latter half of the draw. (The back muscles move the draw shoulder around toward your spine, dragging your folded draw arm with it.) This use of your large back muscles is usually referred to as "using back tension."

A note on back tension: If you are not familiar with this term, it is a technical hot button. It refers to the situation at full draw when you are holding the bow's draw force while aiming and then through the remainder of the shot. This holding is done primarily with the muscles in the upper half of your back. You should be able to feel that those muscles are tensed, hence the term *back (muscle) tension*. There is probably more false information flowing about on this term than any other in archery.

The problem for archers trying to learn how to activate those muscles is that they are not in a position to be used in the first half of the draw (they have no leverage). The back muscles can kick in only in the second half of the draw, but by then you will have mobilized arm and shoulder muscles to get you that far. Those muscles need to be relaxed and the back muscles tensed on the way to full draw. (The reason is simply that you want the muscles responsible for holding to be as far removed as possible from the muscles responsible for releasing the string. That plus the large muscles in your back are more capable of holding the force of your bow without fatiguing than are the smaller muscles in your arm and shoulder.) Don't worry, we have included some drills to help you figure out how to do this. And then you can check one of archery's mysteries off your list!

Follow Through

To follow through in archery, at the end of your shot, means simply maintaining your full draw body position through the end of a shot. Primarily it involves holding your arms up at the levels they were just before the string was released. This has to be trained, but all else is simply reaction (i.e., a followthrough is something that mostly just happens, not something you do). (If you were wondering, "to follow through" is an instruction, while "a followthrough" is the name of the form element.)

In this chapter you will find drills to help you learn your first stance, if you do not yet have one; to help you learn a new stance; or to try out other stances to see how they affect your shot. In subsequent chapters you will find drills to help you refine your stance, to fine-tune it to make it yours and as valuable to you as it can be. The same is true for the other shot elements making up your shot sequence.

It turns out that your shot sequence isn't just a list of things to do. It also provides you with terms you can use when discussing parts of your shot with your coach or fellow archers. Finally, it provides a framework for the mental program you will create to support your shot. For each of your form elements, there are things to think about and things to avoid thinking about. (*Tip:* When shooting, you want to confine your conscious thoughts to what is happening *now*, but more on that later.)

1.1 FINDING YOUR NATURAL STANCE

Purpose

This drill finds the orientation of your stance that puts your body in the position it wants to aim from with a minimum of conflict between parts of your body. It allows your body to feel for a stable full draw position without being controlled by your eyes and mind.

Elite athletes often work one part of their bodies against the resistance of another part. Non-elite athletes are better off avoiding that because things are difficult enough without having one part of your body making it harder for another.

Signs It Is Needed

If you find your aim drifting to one side of the target or the other, or that you are fighting your aim, or if your misses are consistently to one side of center, you may be setting up in a way your body doesn't want.

How to Do It

Stand in front of a target face at some distance with bow and arrow, but do not shoot. Take your normal stance and close your eyes; bring your bow up, draw and anchor and settle in, then open your eyes. If your bow or sight isn't pointed exactly at the vertical centerline of the target (in the left–right sense, not up–down), move your feet until it is. Let down. Repeat this process until you can draw on the target with your eyes closed and then when you open them, you are pointed in the right direction. This is your natural stance.

Variations

Advanced to elite compound archers can expand this drill by shooting at a short distance (up to 20 yards [18 m]). The archer closes the eyes *after taking aim* and then finishes the shot. If the archer's stance is wrong, the arrows will drift left or right of center. If the archer stands on a piece of cardboard taped to the floor, the correct stance can be outlined by a marking pen. As adjustments are made to the stance, each new foot position is highlighted with a different color outline. If the arrows tend to leave the center to the left, the stance needs to be turned to the right, and vice versa. The cardboard can then be used as a template for practice until the new stance is second nature.

Tips

This procedure needs to be repeated from time to time because the stance could change after injuries or weight gain or other effects. If you change your stance in any way and want a natural stance, do the drill again.

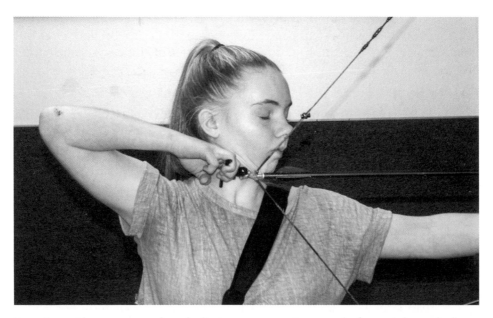

Drawing with your eyes closed eliminates corrections made from sight and allows your body to find its natural position.

Purpose

This drill helps you evaluate whether a different stance will work better for you.

Signs It Is Needed

Most archers start with an even, or square, stance, but you will not be able to appreciate a better stance unless you try others. The goal for a stance is to allow you to be still at full draw. Target archery is shot on flat fields, but field archery may need uphill, downhill, or sidehill stances, so more than one stance is needed.

How to Do It

There are two parts: orientation and variation trials. We'll cover orientation here and the variations in the drill that follows. For the orientation part, stand as if shooting, with or without a bow.

1. Starting with your feet together, close your eyes and then raise one foot off the ground. Notice how your balance shifts. Those little twitches you are feeling are made by stabilizer muscles.

2. Now touch the toe of the raised foot to the ground. You will notice your balance improve.

3. Bring both feet back together on the ground, and you will see your balance improve more.

4. Spread your feet sideways until your heels are about shoulder-width apart, and you will see your balance improve again.

5. Spread your feet half again as wide, and you will feel your balance get worse.

6. Now find the foot positions that give you the best balance (best balance = most still at full draw).

Tips

Exploring stances can take a long time. Once you identify a new stance as worth trying, you must shoot many weeks with your new stance to be able to evaluate it. Do you feel steadier at full draw? Do you feel more in control? Have your groups gotten smaller or practice round scores gone up?

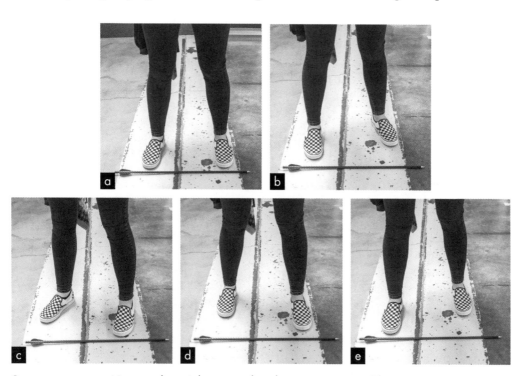

So many stances. You need to pick one and make it your stance. Then you can experiment with the others, using this drill for instance. *(a)* A square stance, *(b)* an open stance, *(c)* a closed stance, *(d)* an oblique stance, and *(e)* another oblique stance. It is recommended that the feet always be in line with the legs as they normally are and not twisted in or out.

1.3 DANCE THE STANCE: VARIATIONS

Purpose

This drill gets you to try other stances so you can evaluate whether a different stance will work better for you. After completing the Dance the Stance: Orientation drill, you can try these variations.

Signs It Is Needed

If you started with an even, or square, stance, you will not be able to appreciate a better stance unless you try others. The goal for a stance is to allow you to be still at full draw when you are executing shots. Target archery is shot on flat fields, but field archery may need uphill, downhill, or sidehill stances, so more than one stance is needed.

How to Do It

There are two parts: orientation (see the Dance the Stance: Orientation drill) and variation trials. These variation trials are best done while shooting and at close range (as are all trials with different form).

1. After warming up, try an open stance.
2. Try a closed stance.
3. Try an oblique stance.

You'll need to shoot more than just a few arrows to get the feel of such stances. You can shoot "blind bale" (i.e., with your eyes closed) while still very close to the target to concentrate on your feeling of being balanced. Also, you can vary the degree of turn (if the stance is being turned), the degree to which the feet are spread apart, or both.

> ### MAKE IT A GAME
>
> Once you have several dozen shots on each of the stances you are trying, you may want to "dance the stance." This involves shooting with a different stance for each arrow. You can have a shooting partner call out the stance you are to use for each shot. You'll want to do this quickly without fussing. After several minutes of this drill ask yourself, "Did any of these feel better to me?" If so, that may be the stance you want to commit to for a while.

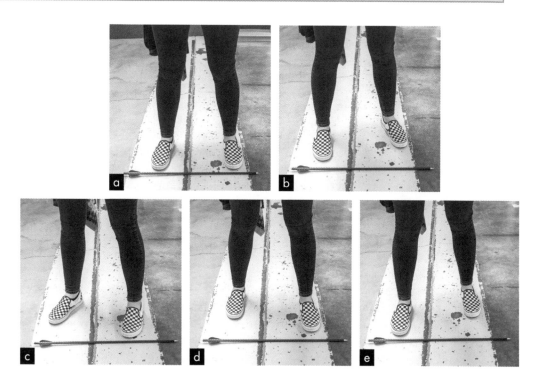

(a) A square stance, *(b)* an open stance, *(c)* a closed stance, *(d)* an oblique stance, and *(e)* another oblique stance. It is recommended that the feet always be in line with the legs as they normally are and not twisted in or out.

Purpose

This drill reinforces consistent bow hand placement on the bow, a requisite for good shooting form.

Signs It Is Needed

If the bow feels different in your hand from shot to shot, consider this drill to make sure your hand placement is consistent.

How to Do It

First, place a piece of masking tape on the front edge of your bow's arrow shelf. Make a pen mark on the center of that piece of tape. Place your hand correctly in your bow and make a mark on your hand (in washable ink) that lines up with the tape mark. Then place your hand in your bow, raise it, and draw to anchor with your eyes closed. Open your eyes and check to see if the marks are aligned. Also check the feel in your bow hand (Did it move? Is it stable?). Repeat as necessary.

Second, experiment with tucking your three bottom fingers alongside your bow to help guide it into position. If you can arrange to have a mirror placed so you can examine your bow hand from the other side, repeat the first part of the drill, and when you open your eyes, check to see whether the tucked fingers are relaxed and in a consistent position. Also check the feel in your bow hand. Repeat as necessary.

Variations

You can use a video camera or smartphone on a tripod in lieu of a mirror. Set them up to record your bow hand, from the other side, while you do a series of repetitions, then play back the video.

Tips

Mounting brackets are made that allow you to attach a smartphone to a tripod.

(a) Tucking the bottom three fingers of your bow hand keeps the fingers from wrapping around the bow. (b) Putting a mark on both the bow and the web of your bow hand allows you to line up the two consistently. (c) Smartphones can very useful for taking video. By using a tripod mount, you can record yourself without needing a camera operator.

1.5 SHOULDERS UP, SHOULDERS DOWN

Purpose

This drill teaches basic shoulder position to beginners.

Signs It Is Needed

Beginners often hunch their bow shoulders to help hold up the bow. This is normal but undesirable because it doesn't align the forces of the bow along the lengths of bones.

How to Do It

Start by standing (no bow) and raising both your shoulders while saying, "Shoulders up," then lowering your shoulders as far as they will drop and saying, "Shoulders down." Do two repetitions, then raise both arms to horizontal from the shoulders-down position.

Variations

Once this drill becomes second nature, proceed from the arms-up position to full draw position by turning your head and bending your draw arm, all with the shoulders down.

(a) Shoulders up! *(b)* Shoulders down! (Repeat both.) *(c)* Raise both arms while keeping the shoulders down. *(d)* Turn the head toward the target, bending the rear arm to anchor.

Tips

A mirror can help. When done right, a notch (called the *acromial notch*) appears atop the shoulders when the arms are raised.

If you have set your shoulder correctly, the acromial notch (see arrow) will be visible. If you have raised your shoulder with your bow arm, it will not be visible.

Purpose

This drill shows how to protect bow arms and elbows from bowstring slaps. The elbow is wider when it is sideways, and this puts the unprotected elbow too close to the path of the bowstring. Rotating the elbow moves the vulnerable region out of the way.

Signs It Is Needed

If your elbow crease is pointed upward rather than toward your bow, or any part of your bow arm is too close to the path of the bowstring (indicated by being hit by the string during shots), you need this drill.

How to Do It

You need an outward-pointing wall corner or a small-diameter post or doorframe to lean against. Place the bow hand on the corner, post, or doorframe as you would on a bow (in good full draw form), lean slightly against the edge, and then rotate the bow elbow back and forth (to establish the range of motion) and then into a safe position (elbow crease is near vertical). During shooting, this rotation is done typically just before the bow is raised.

Tips

The arm geometry of some people is such that the elbow crease faces upward, and this cannot be corrected. A neoprene sleeve can be used to protect the vulnerable elbow until you have enough experience and are able to avoid the string (as you gain experience, the path the bowstring takes becomes more narrow and more regular).

(a) Elbow normally positioned. (b) Elbow rotated. Note: If you cannot get the elbow crease vertical—as this archer cannot—close is good, but avoid too much tension.

1.7 ROTATE THAT ELBOW 2

Purpose

This drill shows how to protect bow arms and elbows from bowstring slaps. The elbow is wider when it is sideways, and this puts the unprotected elbow too close to the path of the bowstring. Rotating the elbow moves the vulnerable region out of the way.

Signs It Is Needed

If your elbow crease is pointed upward rather than toward your bow, or any part of your bow arm is too close to the path of the bowstring (indicated by being hit by the string during shots), you need this drill.

How to Do It

Assume the position of an old-fashioned volleyball player on defense, with your fingers knitted together. Rotate your arms while they are straight without breaking the hold of one hand by the other. Rotate back and forth to the extreme positions.

Once comfortable with the drill, pick up your bow, prepare as if to shoot, rotate your elbow so the crease will be near vertical when the bow is raised, and raise the bow. Check the elbow position. Repeat as necessary.

Tips

The arm geometry of some people is such that the elbow crease faces upward with the bow raised, and this cannot be corrected. A neoprene sleeve can be used to protect the vulnerable elbow until you have enough experience and are able to avoid the string (as you gain experience, the path the bowstring takes becomes more narrow and more regular).

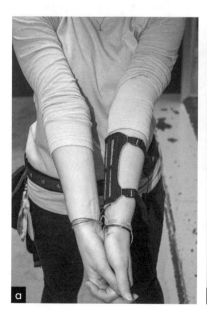
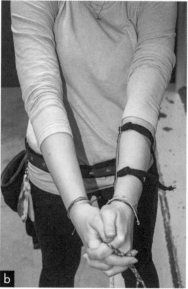

Purpose

This drill helps you learn to raise the bow without raising your shoulders.

Signs It Is Needed

If you hunch either shoulder while raising the bow, your draw length will be affected, which, in turn, affects almost everything else. If you feel this happening, or if your coach or shooting partner notices this, you need to correct it.

How to Do It

You will need a helper. Just before you raise the bow, your helper places a side of a finger on top of each shoulder. If your shoulders rise, the helper is to resist that rise, so you can feel it. Repeat as necessary.

Tips

Instead of placing fingers on top of your shoulders, your helper can place them under your armpits, pressing upward. The task then becomes holding the fingers down. Raising your arms without raising your shoulders will feel odd. If it is not uncomfortable at first, try again.

1.9 DRAW ARM RELAXATION

Purpose

This drill allows archers to perceive by feel what a relaxed draw hand is like.

Signs It Is Needed

Tension in the back of the draw hand is indicated by arching of the hand or wrist and is noticeable by you or an observer (coach, shooting partner).

How to Do It

You will need a helper. Facing each other, each of you makes a deep hook in your string fingers. You then pull (slightly) against the other and then wiggle your hands, wrists, and forearms without losing the connection. Wiggle your helper's arm with your arm relaxed until your helper's arm relaxes. Then say, "This is the feeling I want to have in my forearm, wrist, and hand."

Tips

The muscles making the finger hook are in the upper forearm, not in the hand, which must be relaxed so the string can flick the fingers out of the way rapidly, giving you a clean release.

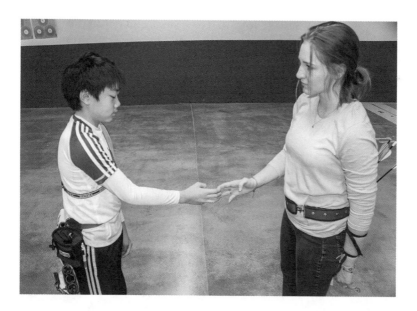

Purpose

This drill provides you with a better idea of what is involved in using your back muscles to draw and hold your bow.

Signs It Is Needed

If your elbow is not straight back, away from the bow, but is "flying" instead, or you feel no involvement of your mid-upper back muscles in the later stages of the draw, you need to learn to engage your back muscles. If your coach or shooting partner sees no or little movement of your scapulae (shoulder blades) during the draw, you need to work on this.

How to Do It

Lie down on carpet or smooth floor, facing up. Using mimetics (play acting) or a stretch band or very light drawing bow, go through the motions of drawing the bow. You should feel considerable movement of your shoulder blades against the floor. After five minutes of this drill, try to achieve the same internal feel while drawing normally (telling you that the right muscles are being used).

Variations

Try drawing with your hand "low" (in this case, closer to your feet) or "high" (in this case, closer to the top of your head). Note the differences in activity in your back muscles.

Tips

If you do this drill on grass, expect major grass stains.

Purpose

This drill provides tactile feedback about the actions of the back muscles used to draw and hold a bow. Transferring the later part of the draw and the hold onto the larger back muscles results in less tension and fatigue in the arm and shoulder muscles.

Signs It Is Needed

If your elbow is not straight back, away from the bow, but is "flying" instead, or you feel no involvement of your mid-upper back muscles in the later stages of the draw, you need to learn to engage your back muscles. If your coach or shooting partner sees no or little movement of your scapulae (shoulder blades) during the draw, you need to work on this.

How to Do It

You will need an assistant. While you draw a light drawing bow or stretch band, have your assistant place their fingertips on your scapulae (shoulder blades). Try to move their fingers together as you draw the bow.

Variations

Alternatively, your assistant can place their thumb or finger between your scapulae, and you try to pinch their thumb or finger between your scapulae. If you have no assistant, you can rest your back against a wall so you can feel the movements in your back.

Purpose

This drill provides you with a better idea of what is involved in using your back muscles to draw your bow.

Signs It Is Needed

If your elbow is not straight back, away from the bow, but is "flying" instead, or you feel no involvement of your mid-upper back muscles in the later stages of the draw, you need to learn to engage your back muscles. If your coach or shooting partner sees no or little movement of your scapulae (shoulder blades) during the draw, you need to work on this.

How to Do It

Stand making a letter T. Bend both arms at the elbow. Try to touch your elbows together behind your back. Focus on the feeling of muscle tension in the mid to upper back and the stretching feeling in front near both shoulders. Both feelings should be present while shooting.

Variations

Alternatively, clasp one wrist with the other hand behind your back and then try to swing both shoulders rearward (without raising them or breaking your grip).

Tips

These back muscles are very strong but aren't used often, so if you are new to archery, go easy because you can develop quite a bit of muscle soreness if you overdo it.

1.13 REVERSALS

Purpose

This drill builds up stamina and strength around drawing and holding your bow at full draw. This common drill is used to build up to a bow of more draw weight than you are currently shooting.

Signs It Is Needed

If you find yourself feeling stressed at full draw or shaking, this drill will be beneficial. If you experience the signs of stress only after you have shot several dozen arrows, then your stamina is in question. If the signs show up immediately, then strength is the issue. *Warning:* There is no surer way to undermine learning than using a bow that is too stout for you. (This is called "being overbowed.")

How to Do It

Proceed through your shot sequence as normal, but upon reaching anchor, begin to count: 1,001, 1,002, 1,003, and so on. You must maintain good full draw position the entire time you are at full draw. If your form degrades, let down and start over.

Start by doing small numbers of repetitions (three to six holds) at full draw in small sets (one to three), with the holds whatever you can manage in length: three seconds, five seconds, and so on. As you feel more comfortable, increase the number of seconds and the number of holds. Elite archers can get up as high as 30 seconds in their sets, but save that for when you are an elite archer.

Tips

You might want to do this drill at the end of a training session so the fatigue it causes won't limit what else you can get done in your session. Also, since you will already be somewhat fatigued at the end of the session, it will make this drill that much more effective.

Safety Note

Do not shoot at the end of a reversal. The fatigue associated with the drill results in unsafe launches of arrows.

Holding . . . 1,001, 1,002, 1,003 . . .

1.14 DOUBLE DRAWS (TRIPLE, TOO!)

Purpose

This drill builds up stamina and strength around drawing your bow. This is a common drill used to build up to a bow of more draw weight.

Signs It Is Needed

If you find yourself feeling stressed at full draw or shaking, this drill will be beneficial. If you experience the signs of stress only after you have shot several dozen arrows, then your stamina is in question. If the signs show up immediately, then strength is the issue. *Warning:* There is no surer way to undermine learning than using a bow that is too stout for you. (This is called "being overbowed.")

How to Do It

Until you are adept at this drill, place your target butt at just a few paces so you cannot miss it. You do not need a target face.

Set up to shoot normally, but after you draw your bow fully, let down to your pre-draw position (some inches of draw still; how many varies with the technique you've chosen to use). Do not let down the bow to brace where there is no pull from the bow. Then you draw again, anchor, and finish the shot.

Start by doing small numbers of repetitions (three to six shots) in small sets (one to three). Rest between sets. As you feel more comfortable, increase the number of shots and the number of sets.

Variations

Once you have gotten comfortable doing double draws, you can move up to triple draws, which incorporate three draws per shot. You can also increase the load by looping a stretch tube or band around your bow and drawing your elbow to increase the effective draw weight of your bow. Start with a light band if trying this until you get used to it.

> ### MAKE IT A GAME
>
> Have a contest with your training partner of 10 shots at a target using double draws to see who gets the better score. Shoot for a prize, maybe a sports drink. Start these competitions at shorter distances until you develop skill. If one of you is a better shot than the other, it is traditional to negotiate a handicap, a number of points to be spotted to the weaker shot.

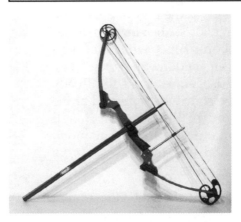

This is a SafeDraw device. It bolts in the place of the arrow rest and acts as somewhat of a stabilizer while it is in use. It allows shooting practice with no arrows involved.

Tips

This same approach can be applied to many other parts of your shot. For example, you can take your stance, then step off the line and take it again before continuing the shot.

(a) After anchoring, letting down to just a few inches of draw and then drawing a second (or third) time is a great strength-building exercise. (b) Looping a stretch band or tube around an archer's bow and draw elbow ramps up the force needed to draw without changing the bow. It is not recommended that you shoot this way; this is just for strength building.

1.15 EXPLORING DIFFERENT ANCHORS

Purpose

This drill shows the effects of having different anchor positions.

Signs It Is Needed

Generally, different anchor positions are used for shooting different distances (low anchors for far targets, high anchors for near). You may need multiple anchor positions if your bow is underpowered for the distances you wish to shoot.

How to Do It

Start up close to a target butt for safety. After warming up shooting, switch to a stretch band and practice using a different anchor. Then shoot arrows with your bow, aiming at the same spot you used for your warm-up. By aiming at the same spot as your warm-up, you can see the effect of each change in anchor position. Generally, the lower the anchor, the higher the hit.

Variations

If you use a low or Olympic anchor, try anchoring with a fingertip in the corner of your mouth. Traditionally, the index fingertip in the corner of your mouth is called the high anchor, but the middle fingertip can be so employed for an even higher anchor, as well as any number of other positions.

Tips

Beginners are almost always started with a high anchor because their target faces are large and close to them. If you work with beginners, this is how you should start them.

MAKE IT A GAME

With or without a bow sight, figure out where to aim to get an arrow to hit the target center. Change the anchor and make some shots. See how many shots are needed to compensate for the anchor change. You can compete with a shooting partner this way. To make the game more difficult over time, move the target butt farther away.

1.16 TRANSFERRING THE LOAD

Purpose

This drill teaches you to unload your arms and shoulders and transfer the force of the bow to your center core, thus moving the load from small muscles to larger, stronger ones.

Signs It Is Needed

Every archer needs to learn how and when to do this. Practicing this valuable process as a drill will make it an automatic part of your shot process.

How to Do It

Start on flat ground at a close distance to a target. Blank bale is preferable in the development stages of this drill; as you get better, you can choose any distance, with or without a target. (Once you can do this quickly, you need to drive your eye acquisition of the target center more quickly.)

As you begin to draw your bow, the smaller muscles in your arms and shoulders become engaged because you are not in position to leverage your back muscles and core. Once at full draw, the load of the bow should move out of your drawing arm and into your back muscles, allowing your drawing arm to unload, or relax (the feeling is much like squeezing your shoulder blades together). The bow arm should hold the load set initially until followthrough is complete.

As you come to anchor and your eye has fully acquired the center of the target, move your conscious effort to unloading your drawing hand and forearm by moving the bulk of the load into your back muscles. Focus your attention on relaxing your hand and forearm as the load moves to your back. Hold this relaxed state through the release and followthrough.

Tips

As you improve your skills with this drill, notice how much more fluid your movements are when coming through the clicker or actuating the release aid because of the absence of tension in the drawing arm at the time of execution. Your shot timing often speeds up as a result. As your shot timing speeds up, faster eye acquisition of the target becomes important to not slow down the process.

Purpose

This drill provides practice relaxing the draw fingers for the release of the string. The muscles making the finger hook are in the upper forearm, not in the hand, which must be relaxed so the string can rapidly flick the fingers out of the way.

Signs It Is Needed

If you are plucking the bowstring (draw hand flying away from your face) while shooting or you feel muscle tension in your draw hand, you need this drill.

How to Do It

You will need a couple of thin plastic bags with handle holes in them (these are often used by grocery stores to bag moist items). Place a couple of water bottles in a bag (you can double that number for more weight), and allow the bag to hang at your side. Place the bag handles where your string goes on your fingers. Allow the bag to release from your fingers by relaxing them. You are looking for a clean drop of the bag, with your fingers ending in a curled, relaxed position. To save wear and tear on the bags, drop them on something soft, like a cushion.

Variations

You can substitute a plastic pail with a wire bail on it. Place several heavier objects in the pail (rocks or bricks) to simulate the weight at full draw, and do the drill as described. The goal is to get the bottom of the bucket to hit the floor squarely, which produces quite a loud sound. (If the loose is sloppy, one edge will hit first and the sound will not be as loud.)

Tips

The back of your draw hand should feel as if it is stretching. (It isn't, it just should feel that way.)

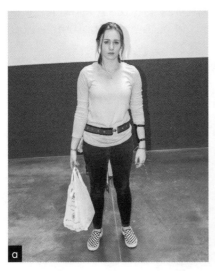
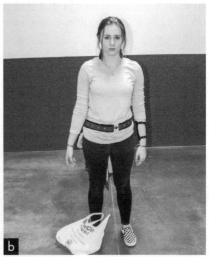

Purpose

This drill provides practice relaxing the draw fingers for the release of the string. The muscles making the finger hook are in the upper forearm, not in the hand, which must be relaxed so the string can rapidly flick the fingers out of the way.

Signs It Is Needed

If you are plucking the bowstring (draw hand flying away from your face) while shooting or you feel muscle tension in your draw hand, you need this drill.

How to Do It

Make a relatively short loop from some rubber tubing (less than half of your draw length). Adopt full draw position, and while stretching the loop release it. The goal is to have the loop fly away in a straight line from the direction it was held in stretched position. If it flies left or right of that line, the release was incorrect.

Variations

You can use a looped stretch band in place of the rubber tubing. Some people like to add a loop of string to the band to place their fingers on to make a more realistic feel at full draw.

Purpose

This drill provides practice relaxing the draw fingers for the release of the string. The muscles making the finger hook are in the upper forearm, not in the hand, which must be relaxed so the string can rapidly flick the fingers out of the way.

Signs It Is Needed

If you are plucking the bowstring (draw hand flying away from your face) while shooting or you feel muscle tension in your draw hand, you need this drill.

How to Do It

Stand a strung recurve bow or longbow on your shoe top. Set your draw fingers into your string hook, hook onto the end serving or string near the top limb tip, pull slightly, then relax the hook. Your hand should come away in a relaxed state, with your fingers slightly curled.

1.20 BEING STILL

Purpose

This drill shows you how your stillness varies during shots. It teaches archers that there is a window in time during which shots score best. This window varies with your archery fitness level. If there is significant movement during the shot, arrow groups expand and scores suffer. Movement needs to be minimized because it cannot be eliminated (humans are never perfectly still).

How to Do It

This drill requires a target butt for safety but does not need to be done at a range. Start with a basic bow with no stabilizers or bow sight.

Standing right in front of a target butt (for safety), draw your bow and observe the arrow's point. Initially it will move about in quite a jitter. Then it will enter a phase in which the movement is much smaller. After several more seconds, the point's movement will increase. Count how many seconds the point is at its minimum level of movement. Let down at the end. It is from this period of relative stillness that you want to shoot. Shooting earlier or later than that will result in poorer arrow scores.

This drill can be combined with doing reversals.

Variations

After some experience with this drill, add your bow sight and stabilizers to see their effects. With a bow sight attached, focus on the aperture instead of the arrow point.

Tips

This drill should be repeated from time to time. As you gain skill and archery fitness, the period during which you are still will expand and can be used as a gauge of your archery fitness.

MAKE IT A GAME

You can compete with yourself by repeating the drill five times while trying to get each subsequent still period to be longer. You can compete with a shooting partner by seeing who can create the longest still period over five tries.

1.21 BLANK BALE DRILL (RECURVE)

Purpose

Removing the distraction of the target allows you to concentrate on how your shot feels and what your rhythm is like, making those things easier to recognize when shooting.

Signs It Is Needed

If your shot seems too variable or needs to be tightened up, this is the drill for you. (*Hint:* Most archery practice shooting is done blank bale.)

How to Do It

Blank bale is shooting at an archery butt that has no target face, usually at very close distance (two or three paces). Because you are so close, you must be careful to move your arrow hits around the whole face of the butt so you do not accidentally damage arrows in the butt with later shots.

Pick a shot element you want to focus your attention on (e.g., your release). Shoot arrows in succession, focused on what you want to happen. You must focus intensely; do not let your mind wander. After 5 to 10 minutes, you can switch to another form element you wish to work on. Work on only one thing at a time, though.

Tips

If you are practicing for indoor shooting, you can place the butt at shoulder level. If practicing for longer shots outdoors, place the butt somewhat higher in order to adopt the angle your body will typically be at when at full draw.

Some people stick two-inch-round (5 cm) or smaller colored stickers all over the butt to aim at, eliminating the possibility of damaging arrows already in the butt.

If you have very limited training time and can set up to shoot at your home, you will reduce not only walking time back and forth to the target but also travel time back and forth to your archery practice range.

1.22 BLIND BALE DRILL (RECURVE)

Purpose

By removing the distraction of vision, blind bale drills allow you to concentrate on how your shots feel; you will eventually memorize these aspects so they will become managed subconsciously while your conscious mind's attention is consumed with aiming.

Signs It Is Needed

If your shot seems too variable or needs to be tightened up, this is the drill for you.

How to Do It

Blind bale shooting is blank bale shooting done with your eyes closed. Usually you make sure any shot will land on the butt before closing your eyes (for safety). Because you are so close, you must be careful to move your arrow hits around the whole face of the butt so you do not accidentally damage arrows in the butt with later shots.

Pick a shot element you want to focus your attention on (e.g., your anchor point). Shoot arrows in succession, focusing on what you want to happen and identifying how that performance feels. You must focus intensely; do not let your mind wander. After 5 to 10 minutes, you can switch to another form element you wish to work on. Work on only one thing at a time, though.

Tips

If you are practicing for indoor shooting, you can place the butt at shoulder level. If practicing for longer shots outdoors, place the butt somewhat higher so as to adopt the angle your body will typically be at full draw.

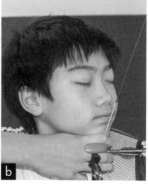

1.23 MIRROR DRILL (RECURVE)

Purpose

This drill allows you to see what you look like in the various phases of your shot sequence. You can identify structural weaknesses in your posture or confirm that you are in the correct body positions, especially full draw position. Frequent quick checks of how your form looks can keep you from drifting off to something quite different in very many tiny increments.

Signs It Is Needed

Beginners and archers feeling out of balance may lean toward or away from the target or up and down the shooting line. In extreme cases, archers sway (i.e., move back and forth between two extreme body positions). All of these can be picked up in mirrors.

How to Do It

An inexpensive closet mirror bought from a hardware store works well. The mirror has to be placed vertically and aligned so you can get visual feedback on your posture.

You can use straight mimetics (also called *miming*) or a stretch band to work through your shot sequence to match the feels from your body to the actual body positions. (The "feel" and the "real" are rarely the same.) For example, at full draw, aiming at the mirror, recurve archers should be able to see any artwork on the back of their shirts because the shoulder line points to the bow, about 10 to 12 degrees to the arrow line.

Safety Note

You can use your bow even up to drawing and aiming at the mirror, but to prevent accidently shooting the mirror and creating flying shards of glass, we recommend not using an arrow.

Tips

If you have a video camera and a tripod (even a smartphone and a tripod adapter for it), you can use it to see aspects of your form you cannot see in mirrors.

1.24 AIMING OFF OF THE BOW HAND

Purpose

This drill steadies the bow arm through the release, avoiding the form flaw of dropping the bow arm.

Signs It Is Needed

If, as you tire, you see arrows hitting lower and lower on the target, or your coach or shooting partner notices your bow arm dropping too quickly after the loose, you need this drill.

How to Do It

Take your bow sight and stabilizers off your bow. At close range and with a blank butt, draw on the butt and align the top knuckle of your bow hand with a spot on the target. (A small sticker can be affixed to the butt to aim at.) The objective is to shoot without losing the alignment of the knuckle with the spot on the butt.

Tips

Move the arrows around as you shoot to avoid damaging arrows already in the butt.

> ### MAKE IT A GAME
>
> Set yourself a goal of how many times in a row you do the drill correctly. If you make the goal, you win. Set another goal for how many times you can meet that goal in one 5- to 10-minute session.

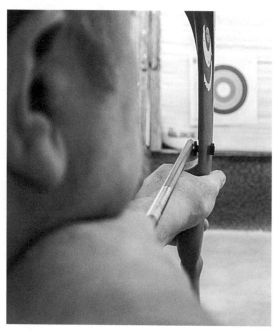

Move the top knuckle of your bow hand until it lines up with a visible mark on the butt. The object of the game is to shoot arrows while keeping that knuckle lined up, keeping it in place throughout the shots.

Purpose

This drill helps you correct your archery posture so you are shooting from a strong base.

Signs It Is Needed

If you lean or sway while shooting, or an observer (coach, shooting partner) notices you are not standing straight, this drill allows you to correct those form flaws.

How to Do It

You will need a helper. The drill can be done shooting and nonshooting. It is probably safest to start off nonshooting.

Your helper has a stick (or a rod, or an arrow) that they will use to touch a spot that needs to be moved (move away from the touch). So if you are leaning away from the target, the helper will touch the stick against your away side, causing you to move toward standing straight.

Variations

Start with a low draw weight bow, then move up to your personal bow. Start with non-shooting and then progress to shooting; when shooting corrections to posture are made after full draw is achieved, then the shot is finished.

Tips

For head position changes, having the helper use a finger-tip is recommended (a stick being waved around your head can be unsettling).

Purpose

This drill allows you to monitor your execution as you move through the postures of a shot.

Signs It Is Needed

If an observer notices that your form changes from shot to shot, you need to learn to monitor these movements through feel.

How to Do It

This is a nonshooting drill. You will need a mirror (best if it can be mounted on a stand of some kind). Position the mirror so it is plumb (slanted mirrors give distorted images), it is in the position of a target, and you can see yourself. Raise your bow, draw, and anchor while observing your reflection in the mirror. Are you standing straight up and down, not leaning left or right? Are your body positions consistent from repetition to repetition?

Variations

Reposition the mirror so it is opposite your chest. Repeat the exercise. (You will need to leave your head looking toward the mirror.)

Reposition the mirror so it is 45 degrees from being in the target direction (between the first two positions) but still vertical. Repeat the process.

Tips

You can substitute a video camera or smartphone on a tripod for a mirror. Set the device to record, and then go through the drills. Since the camera can also record audio, talk to the camera, sharing your observations. Replay the video images to see what you can see in them. Share them with your coach if appropriate.

This drill is also suitable for compound and traditional archers.

1.27 STRING ALIGNMENT

Purpose

This drill builds the important habit of aligning the string with the same exact place on the bow or target from shot to shot.

Signs It Is Needed

Left and right misses on otherwise perfectly good shots often indicate this is your problem.

How to Do It

It doesn't matter where you choose to align the string in the sight of your aiming eye. (You can tune in any reasonable sight picture.) The important thing is that every shot is done the exact same way. The following are popular locations for the string image:

1. The edge of the sight window.
2. The right or left edge of your sight pin aperture.
3. A location on the target face such as the edge of the spot.

Once you have chosen a location you can see and re-create easily, practice for 5 to 10 minutes drawing to anchor and creating this sight picture and then letting down. Rest in between repetitions.

Once you can easily create this sight picture, shoot arrows, focusing on using this sight picture.

Variations

Try different locations for the string image in your sight picture, and find the one that is easiest for you to see and do quickly. Also note how the arrow hits the target in a different spot with different sight pictures.

Tips

Some archers move their string alignment to accommodate for light breezes rather than moving their aperture or aiming off. That way if the wind stops or changes, adjustments do not involve remembering sight windage changes. You must practice this and get good at it to be able to do it.

When your aperture is on target, use your aiming eye to note the position of the string against the background. (It will be out of focus.) The two most commonly used positions are on either side of the aperture (shown), but any part of the bow—or even the target—can be used.

Chapter 2

Compound Essentials

We have separated drills primarily for recurve and longbow archers from those for compound archers because the draw cycles are so different for these two classes of bows. We note the drills that apply to both, but most of the drills in this group are not easily adapted to use with recurve bows and vice versa.

Just as in recurve and longbow archery, it is important to focus first on learning solid basic technique for shooting your compound bow and to make sure you have a clear idea of what kind of shot you are trying to build, so some guidance is necessary. It is beyond the scope of this book to provide a complete component on how to shoot, but here is a short introduction to the form that applies to these kinds of bows.

A STEP-BY-STEP APPROACH

The general approach to learning archery technique is to list the steps, also called *form elements*, involved in making a shot. All together, this is called your *shot sequence*, or *shot routine*. Here is an example:

Basic Shot Sequence

1. Take your stance.
2. Nock an arrow.
3. Attach your release aid.
4. Set your hands.
5. Raise the bow.
6. Draw the string.
7. Find your anchor.
8. Aim.
9. Release the string.
10. Follow through.

With your equipment in hand, following these steps will result in a shot. To make it a good shot, the steps need to be done correctly and in order, and therein lies the task: how to learn a shot sequence so it supports making consistently good shots.

We cover some foundational shot sequence information and expand on three of the form steps in chapter 1 (so you can read about those there), and we will expand on a couple more here.

Aim

Because of the construction of compound bows, the force needed to draw the bow ramps up rapidly, reaches a peak, and then falls off to a small fraction of the peak weight. This let-off of the force needed to hold the bow fully drawn allows compound archers more time to aim, which is a major source of their superior accuracy. Compound archers are also allowed telescopic lenses (called *scopes* in the vernacular) to be used as part of their bow sights (with leveling bubbles built in) as well as peep sights (lozenges inserted into the bowstring with an angled hole in them to be used as a rear sight). Because of all these features, more time is needed to align the apertures (in peep and sight), make sure the bubble level indicates the bow is being held straight up and down, and make sure the aperture dot or ring is centered on the point of aim.

Release the String

Recurve and traditional archers hold the bowstring with their fingers (with a tab or glove as protection from the pressure of the bowstring), but many compound shooting styles allow the use of mechanical release aids (called *releases* in the vernacular). These may be handheld or strapped to your wrist. Some are triggerless (responding to body position or draw force), while others have triggers that are actuated by the thumb or little finger. All releases require training, and you will find drills in this chapter that teach how to use them.

Just as in the previous chapter, you will find drills to help you learn your first stance, if you do not yet have one; to help you learn a new stance; or to try out other stances to see how they affect your shot. In subsequent chapters you will find drills to help you refine your stance, to fine-tune it to make it yours and as valuable to you as it can be. The same is true for the other shot elements making up your shot sequence.

It turns out that your shot sequence isn't just a list of things to do. It also provides you with terms you can use when discussing parts of your shot with your coach or fellow archers. Finally, it provides a framework for the mental program you will create to support your shot. For each of your form elements, there are things to think about and things to avoid thinking about. (*Tip:* When shooting, you want to confine your conscious thoughts to what is happening *now*, but more on that later.)

2.1 FINDING YOUR NATURAL STANCE

Purpose

This drill allows your body to feel for a stable full draw position without being controlled by your eyes and mind. Elite athletes often work one part of their bodies against the resistance of another part in their stances. Non-elite athletes are better off avoiding that, because things are difficult enough without having one part of your body making it harder for another.

Signs It Is Needed

If you find your aim drifting to one side of the target or other, sense that you are fighting your aim, or notice your misses are consistently to one side of center, you may be setting up in a way your body doesn't want.

How to Do It

Stand in front of a target face at some distance with bow and arrow, but do not shoot. Take your stance and close your eyes; bring your bow up, draw and anchor and settle in, then open your eyes. If your bow or sight isn't pointed exactly at the vertical centerline of the target (in the left–right sense, not up–down), move your stance until it is. Let down. Repeat this process until you can draw on the target with your eyes closed and then when you open them, you are pointed in the right direction. This is your natural stance.

Variations

Advanced to elite compound archers can expand this drill by shooting at a short distance (up to 20 yards [18 m]). The archer closes the eyes *after taking aim* and then finishes the shot. If the archer's stance is wrong, the arrows will drift left or right of center. If the archer stands on a piece of cardboard taped to the floor, the correct stance can be outlined by a marking pen. As adjustments are made to the stance, each new foot position is highlighted with a different color outline. If the arrows tend to leave the center to the left, the stance needs to be turned to the right, and vice versa. The cardboard can then be used as a template for practice until the new stance is second nature.

Tips

This procedure needs to be repeated from time to time because the stance could change after injuries or weight gain or other effects. If you change your stance in any way and want a natural stance, do the drill again.

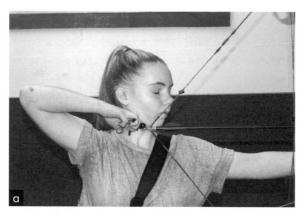 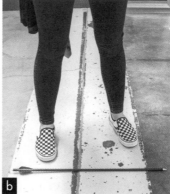

(a) Be sure to keep your finger off the trigger of your release while doing this drill; otherwise loose shots could happen. *(b)* Instead of trying to memorize the stance you come up with, you can use a piece of cardboard with a piece of tape for a shooting line to mark the stances and then use this as a template.

2.2 REFINING YOUR STANCE

Purpose

This drill helps refine your stance, making it more personal and allowing you to train in any changes.

Signs It Is Needed

If you find yourself fighting your aim, trying to stay on target but tending to drift off, you probably need to adjust your stance.

How to Do It

This drill is most easily done indoors. You will need a large square of cardboard, large enough so you can take your stance on it (3 feet [1 m] square). Draw a wide line down the middle (or use a piece of tape). Lay the cardboard on the shooting line so that the line or tape on the cardboard is directly over the shooting line.

Shoot until you are warmed up and shooting good groups. After shooting several such groups, squat down and draw an outline around your shoe tips. Label this "Normal." From this point onward, you can adjust your stance to something slightly different (feet wider apart, heel line at a different angle to the target, and so on). Again, squat down and outline your shoe tips. Shoot using this stance for several practice sessions. (Yes, you need to carry the cardboard around with you.)

Focus on how easily you hold on target and whether you tend to drift off. If you drift off to the left, your body is tending to turn left, so adjust your stance by turning left a bit, and vice versa.

Tips

Having different colored marking pens is quite helpful.

Purpose

This drill shows you where to raise your bow to spend the minimum time at full draw when shooting, thus saving energy.

Signs It Is Needed

If you need to move your bow much once you have achieved full draw, this drill will help minimize those movements.

How to Do It

After warming up, prepare to shoot—but after you raise the bow and before you draw, align your sight aperture (or arrow point) with the center of the target. Then close your eyes, draw and anchor, and then open your eyes. What is your aperture aligned with now? If it started dead center and ended up at 5 o'clock in the blue, then the act of drawing and anchoring moved your bow down and to the right. Therefore, if you were to start your draw up and to the left (at 11 o'clock in the blue), that motion should leave you in the center naturally. (The spot is always an equal distance from the other side of dead center, same color, or same ring six hours away.)

Do the drill several times to locate how your aperture or point moves during draw and anchor, and then try shooting by starting from the revised point (not the center, but your equivalent to 11 o'clock in the blue). If you are consistent, you should be aligned on center or very close to it at anchor. Shoot some arrows to see where your group forms.

Tips

Optional: This starting spot for your aperture or point is fairly consistent at many distances because as the distance to the target increases, so does the target face size. Test this out by using your new starting point at various distances.

If you adopt this as part of your shot sequence, it will become almost automatic.

MAKE IT A GAME

Once you are comfortable with your preliminary point of aim, you can make a game out of it by doing the drill three times or more, but starting on your new preliminary point of aim instead of the center. When you open your eyes, note the position of your sight aperture or arrow point relative to the target face, and score that position as if your arrow had landed there. The goal is a perfect score, but anything close to that is very, very good.

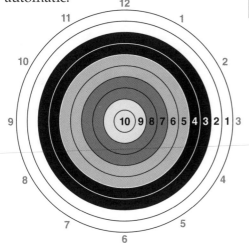

We use analog clock markings to provide descriptions of the landing or sighting areas on target faces—for example, "8 o'clock in the blue" or "4 o'clock in the 6-ring."

Purpose

This drill will help you develop a bulletproof bow arm. This is truly one of the most important drills for improving your scores.

Signs It Is Needed

You feel yourself collapse on the front end. You find your bow arm softens as the day goes on. You struggle to keep the same load in your bow arm from shot to shot.

How to Do It

This drill can be done at any shooting distance, with or without a mirror for visual feedback. On the shooting line, start off with your front and rear shoulders low. Relax and let them fall with gravity to their lowest physical point. While keeping your front shoulder down, place your bow hand in the grip deliberately in your favorite position, with the bow pointed at 45 degrees to the ground. Begin to draw the string. In the beginning of the drawing phase, push gently to the ground and give a gentle engagement of the triceps muscle on your bow arm. With the bow hand relaxed and the bow arm firm, raise your arm and finish the draw phase, holding a mild engagement of the triceps muscle while keeping the front shoulder down in the process.

Recurve archers should hold the mild engagement, while compound archers can relax the triceps once anchor has occurred. The key is to establish an effective energy level in the bow arm in the very beginning and maintain it through the end of the shot and followthrough.

Tips

Include this drill in your daily shooting regimen. Your overall energy will stay with you through your entire round, and your execution control and timing will improve. Adjust the engagement of the triceps muscle to your liking. Some prefer a firm engagement, while others prefer a milder engagement. Play with it to find your sweet spot. The goal is to maximize your skeletal foundation and reduce the use of your muscles to hold or overcome the bow's load. The other key element is that being consistent in the front end or bow arm aids greatly in becoming consistent on the drawing end.

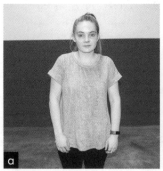
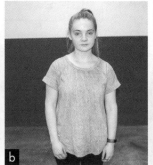

It is normal for your shoulders to rise when you raise your arms. But archers do not do this while shooting.

2.5 BOW SHOULDER SETTING

Purpose

This drill will help you link your bow arm to your core, strengthening and stabilizing your bow arm.

Signs It Is Needed

Everybody needs the benefits of this drill. The consistent placement and use of the bow shoulder directly affects the stability and control of the bow arm and ultimately the shot execution. The bow arm controls clearance and timing, promotes balance, and is a source of stability in windy conditions.

How to Do It

This drill can be done at any distance, with or without a mirror. Practice it at different distances to develop equal control at different body angles.

On the shooting line, start with both arms hanging at your side. Take a deep breath and relax your core and shoulders to the point you can feel them drop as you exhale. Shift about 60 percent of your weight to your front foot. Raise your bow arm, keeping the shoulder down and relaxed. Rotate to the target to your desired position and string clearance. Recurve archers often prefer to rotate the shoulder inward to the point of pronating the front shoulder toward the bow string, while compound archers rarely share this preference. The key is to land any rotation in the exact same spot. A visual reference is a big help (use a mirror to check your form). Once you achieve your desired rotation to the target, give a slight reach to the target from the shoulder—this important step for setting the shoulder should be maintained throughout the entire shot.

Tips

If you are a field or 3-D archer, practice this drill at uphill and downhill angles to improve your game. It is challenging to get the 60:40 weight distribution when shooting uphill. Keeping the shoulder low and relaxed on downhill shots is equally challenging but rewarding.

2.6 INTRODUCTION TO RELEASE TECHNIQUE

Purpose

Using a rope bow or training aid to learn or refine release aid technique removes any danger of prematurely tripping an unfamiliar release aid and incurring injuries. It also allows you to focus on the feel of a successful loose using the release aid without the distraction of the bow and arrow.

Safety Note

There are many styles of mechanical release aids. Variations include hand-held models and models that attach to your wrist. Some are triggerless; others have triggers that you actuate with an index finger, a thumb, or a little finger. Whichever release you have chosen, it must be the proper size for your body. The draw length of your bow may need to be adjusted to account for the shape and position of the release aid at full draw and of a D-loop if one has just been installed. After all that, the technique must be learned and practiced safely. This is what these drills provide.

Signs It Is Needed

If you are shooting a release aid for the first time or are changing from one style of release aid to another, you need to train in your new release. A premature release of a compound bow being drawn can result in the draw hand flying back wildly, which can damage an archer's face.

> ### MAKING A ROPE BOW
>
> Using strong cord (we use 3/16-inch polypropylene rope), cut a length more than twice your draw length. (Melt the ends with a propane lighter to keep them from fraying. *Warning:* Touching melted plastic can result in severe burns. Let it cool!) Line up the two cut ends and tie a single overhand (shoelace) knot, making a loop. Reposition the knot to make the draw length of the loop match that of your bow.
>
> Carry this with you; release archers are always borrowing releases to try.
>
>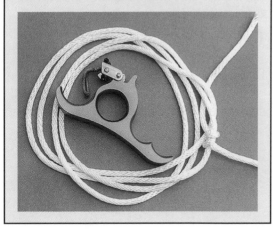

How to Do It

You will need a rope bow (see the Making a Rope Bow box). Fit this loop to the length that when looped around your bow hand (where the bow normally goes), the release is held at the desired anchor position. This is easily done by moving the knot making the loop or adding knots until the loop is just the right size.

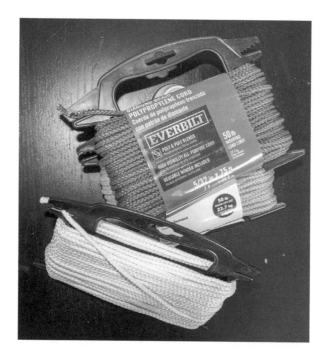

2.7 FINDING YOUR RELEASE ANCHOR POSITION

Purpose

Using a rope bow or training aid to learn or refine release aid technique removes any danger of prematurely tripping an unfamiliar release aid and incurring injuries. It also allows you to focus on the feel of a successful loose using the release aid without the distraction of the bow and arrow.

Safety Note

There are many styles of mechanical release aids. Variations include hand-held models and models that attach to your wrist. Some are triggerless; others have triggers that you actuate with an index finger, a thumb, or a little finger. Whichever release you have chosen, it must be the proper size for your body. The draw length of your bow may need to be adjusted to account for the shape and position of the release aid at full draw and the addition of a D-loop if one has just been installed. After all that, the technique must be learned and practiced safely. This is what these drills provide.

Signs It Is Needed

If you are shooting a release aid for the first time or are changing from one style of release aid to another, you need to find a comfortable, repeatable anchor position for your release hand.

How to Do It

You will need a rope bow (see the Introduction to Release Technique drill for how to make one). To find your anchor position, attach your release aid to the loop, arrange the loop over your bow hand, and assume a full draw position. Apply just enough tension to the loop for everything to feel stable. Then rotate your release hand around the axis of your forearm as far as it will go toward your face and then away. The position you are looking for is exactly halfway between the two most extreme positions. This is the most relaxed position for your hand and forearm. Repeat as necessary until you can find that position comfortably and quickly.

Eventually you will transition to shooting arrows from your bow (see the variations in drill 2.8). When first shooting arrows, be sure to draw slightly out of line with your face in case of an accidental release. If you experience any difficulties (e.g., flinching, stalling, punching), go back to practicing with the rope bow or training aid until you feel comfortable using the release, then try your bow again.

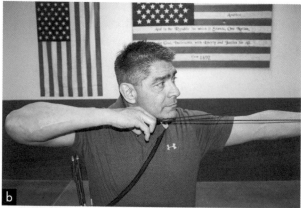

All the way around one way, then all the way around the other, and then right in the middle. Typically the back of the hand makes an angle of 10 to 15 degrees to the ground.

2.8 HONING YOUR RELEASE TECHNIQUE

Purpose

Using a rope bow or training aid to learn or refine release aid technique removes any danger of prematurely tripping an unfamiliar release aid and incurring injuries. It also allows you to focus on the feel of a successful loose using the release aid without the distraction of the bow and arrow.

Safety Note

There are many styles of mechanical release aids. Variations include hand-held models and models that attach to your wrist. Some are triggerless; others have triggers that you actuate with an index finger, a thumb, or a little finger. Whichever release you have chosen, it must be the proper size for your body. The draw length of your bow may need to be adjusted to account for the shape and position of the release aid at full draw and the addition of a D loop if one has just been installed. After all that, the technique must be learned and practiced safely. This is what these drills provide.

How to Do It

You will need a rope bow (see the Introduction to Release Technique drill for how to make one). Once you have identified your best full draw position (see the Finding Your Release Anchor Position drill), attach the release to your rope bow, arrange the loop over your bow hand, assume your full draw position, and pull hard enough to simulate the holding weight of your bow. Actuate the release using the best technique for your style of release. The rope should fly out of your hand away from the direction of the pull to land on the floor roughly one pace away. If it doesn't, try again. If it does, after a half dozen successful trials, most people hang onto the loop rather than having to bend over and pick it up all the time.

Eventually you will transition to shooting arrows from your bow (see the variations). When first shooting arrows, be sure to draw slightly out of line with your face in case of an accidental release. If you experience any difficulties (e.g., flinching, stalling, punching), go back to practicing with the rope bow or training aid until you feel comfortable using the release, then try your bow again.

Variations

Once you have achieved success with the rope bow, there are several things you can try before attempting shots with your bow. There are training aids made to supply a source of holding weight (e.g., a Genesis bow with a SafeDraw training aid attached, a Saunders Firing-Line release trainer). A stretch band with a cord loop attached (to be able to attach the release) provides more dynamic simulation of shots.

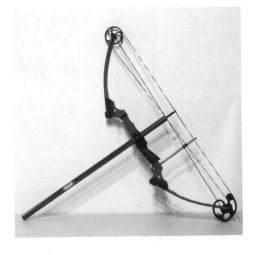

Purpose

This drill teaches you the correct method for activating a handheld trigger-less release aid.

Signs It Is Needed

If your release is inconsistent or an observer (coach, shooting partner) can see you manipulating the release body, you need this drill.

How to Do It

For this drill, the key to success is building the muscle–nerve pathways that automatically perform the correct activation method. Start by shooting up close (10 paces or less) without the distraction of a target so you can focus on your body. Then hit full draw and take a moment to acquire the sight and the target (because you will always do this when shooting at a target). Once comfortable with your sight picture, relax your drawing hand and gently pull with your back muscles until the release goes off.

When done correctly, there is no additional load to the drawing hand or arm. In fact, quite the opposite occurs. The tension should run out of the hand and arm and into the back and core. You will find that the release goes off quickly and with minimal effort.

Variations

If using a thumb-triggered release "back-tension style," place your thumb on the trigger and then relax the drawing hand and pull with your back.

Once you are comfortable doing this drill with blank bales, put up a target face and include aiming in the drill.

Tips

If the release doesn't trip at the correct moment, you may need to adjust that feature of the release aid. It should be set up so that the release trips when your draw elbow is pointing directly away from the target.

If you need a little more effort to make the release go off, place the effort on the middle finger. Incorporating a little load transfer to the center or middle finger will speed up the shot.

2.10 WRIST STRAP RELEASE ACTIVATION

Purpose

This drill teaches you the correct method to activate a wrist strap release aid.

Signs It Is Needed

If your release is inconsistent or an observer (coach, shooting partner) can see you punching your release, you need this drill. No movement of the trigger finger should be visible.

How to Do It

This style of release aid is the most popular for hunting because of its fast and simple engagement to the string (and you can't drop it). A few target archers successfully use them in competition. In either case, it is important to build the habit of triggering the release as a surprise with a deliberate method.

Start up close with no target so you can focus on your body movement rather than the sight and target. As you attach the release, move your trigger finger away from the trigger to avoid accidental contact (usually it is placed behind the trigger).

Come to full draw and anchor. Acquire your sight picture. Now move your finger around and onto the trigger avoiding using the finger pad at all. To activate the trigger, simply engage your back muscles and swing your draw elbow around until the release goes off. It should go off absent of any change in the trigger finger pressure.

Variations

Adjust the speed of the shot by the amount of load you start your trigger finger with (by squeezing off part of the force needed to trip the release).

Tips

If the release doesn't trip at the correct moment, you may need to adjust that feature of the release aid. It should be set up so that the release trips when your draw elbow is pointing directly away from the target.

Place your finger on the trigger at different depths or locations to find the most comfortable spot. Some prefer the fingertip, while others prefer to wrap to the first knuckle. Although making this change often requires some adjustment of the release itself in how it fits you, it is worth doing to find the place where you feel you have the greatest level of control.

2.11 DRAWING MOTION

Purpose

This drill will help you develop perfect upper-body rotation and shoulder alignment with the target.

Signs It Is Needed

You or an observer (coach, shooting partner) finds that your shoulder alignment to the target varies from shot to shot. (The shoulder line should be parallel to your arrow at full draw.)

How to Do It

This drill can be done at any distance, with or without a target. Drawing while facing a mirror (without an arrow, for safety) so you can see what your final alignment looks like is helpful.

The starting position of your shoulders for drawing is always out of line. As you rotate to full draw, a shoulder alignment occurs (in recurve or longbow, the shoulder line typically points to the bow; in compound, it points to the target). Emphasize getting the line of your shoulders to point where you desire as early in the draw phase as possible, and hold it there. (Usually this is somewhere in the second half of your draw phase.) This movement should be absent of tension (i.e., move into that position without force).

Variations

As with all mirror drills, you can use a video camera or smartphone instead, with the benefit that you can share the videos with your coach. With a camera running, you can also do this drill with your eyes closed and then check the video to see if your "feel" for the situation is true.

Tips

The emphasis needs to be on the rotation of your torso needed to pull the bow and achieving the final resting place of your rear or drawing shoulder.

The shoulder line (a) points off to the side before the draw and (b) points to the target when you have completed the draw and anchor. If this is not the case, a draw length adjustment or form adjustment is necessary.

2.12 DRAWING ELBOW POSITION

Purpose

This drill teaches you what it feels like to be in the correct position on your drawing side (having *good alignment* or *good line*). When in the proper position, you maximize the use of leverage and body position, allowing for a more relaxed shot (because fewer muscles are used). This drill provides the feedback through touch.

Safety Note

Do not shoot arrows during this drill; the focus behind you may result in fliers.

Signs It Is Needed

Most of us need this drill.

How to Do It

This drill requires a helper. Do this drill at 20 yards (18 m) or so. Have your helper place their hand where your drawing elbow should wind up at full draw (like a bumper to stop the elbow). This provides a reference as to how far to go.

Draw your bow and move your rear shoulder and scapula toward your spine (keeping the shoulder low), anchor, and expand until you are able to bump the hand of your helper. Most people find they stop short and do not properly rotate the scapula to the spine, creating a loss of leverage and requiring additional muscle support and engagement to make up for the loss.

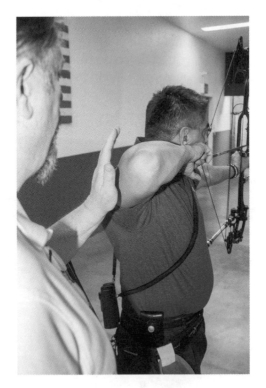

Tips

As you do this drill, imagine yourself moving your elbow into your partner's hand, as opposed to pulling the bow to their hand. The goal is to build a memory of your best body position, as opposed to pulling the string excessively. Move the drawing shoulder and scapula to make the contact instead of pulling the string and increasing draw length.

This drill is equally important for compound and recurve archers.

2.13 AIMING ON CENTER

Purpose

This drill builds quicker target acquisition to prevent wasted time and energy at full draw. The goal is to teach yourself to stay locked on the target rather than have wandering focal points.

Signs It Is Needed

If you struggle to acquire the target and find that your aiming eye wanders during the shot process, this is one of the most important drills to master.

How to Do It

Start up close with a large target face. Practice acquiring the target in the very beginning of your drawing sequence, and stay locked on your point of aim. The goal is not just to find the central ring but to acquire the center of the center. This can be done without shooting the arrow but should transition to shooting fairly soon.

Practice keeping your focus on the center starting at the beginning of the draw cycle, during the holding process, and during the entire followthrough—even through the arrow's hitting the target. Exaggerate holding your focus on the middle for as long as you can, well after the arrow is gone and in the target. You will find that in the beginning this is not an easy drill to do, and your eyes and focus tend to shut off when the bow goes off, but through practicing this drill you will get better and faster.

Tips

From time to time try both focal points, the target and the sight, back and forth during the same shot. One will be easier to do than the other. This will reinforce why you chose the method you did and remind you to stay with it.

SHOULD I FOCUS ON THE APERTURE OR ON THE TARGET?

There are two schools of thought on the correct method to aim using a sight. Some archers prefer to focus on the sight pin or scope while the target is a blur (out of focus), but most prefer to focus on the target and allow the pin or scope to be out of focus. We recommend you try both and pick one and stick with it.

Whichever your preferred method, the goal is to be consistent. Because your eyes and the associated brain functions (e.g., visual cortex) are very powerful and are capable of instantly processing a great amount of information, it takes real effort to achieve maximum control when you need it. Having complete control of target acquisition is of paramount importance to an archer's consistency. Equally important is to stay locked on your focus point for the entire shot process.

2.14 MIRROR DRILL (COMPOUND)

Purpose

This drill allows you to see what you look like in the various phases of your shot sequence. Any out-of-position body parts can be corrected. Frequent quick checks of how your form looks can keep you from drifting off to something quite different through very many tiny changes.

Signs It Is Needed

Beginners and archers feeling out of balance may be leaning toward or away from the target or up and down the shooting line. In extreme cases archers sway (i.e., move back and forth between two extreme body positions).

How to Do It

An inexpensive closet mirror bought from a hardware store works well. The mirror has to be placed vertically and aligned so you can get visual feedback on your posture.

You can use straight mimetics or a stretch band to work through your shot sequence to match the feels from your body to the actual body positions. (The "feel" and the "real" are rarely the same.) For example, at full draw while aiming at the mirror, compound archers should be able to see that their shoulder line is parallel with their arrow line.

Safety Note

You can use your bow even up to drawing and aiming at the mirror, but we recommend not using an arrow so you will not accidently shoot the mirror and create flying shards of glass. This can, however, be done safely if your release aid has a lockout that prevents your release from tripping off a shot.

If you have a bow equipped with a SafeDraw or similar shot trainer, you can execute shots while looking into the mirror to see what happens after the release. (Which way does your bow hand move? Your release hand? Your head?)

Variations

If you have a video camera and a tripod (even a smartphone and a tripod adapter for it), you can use it to see aspects of your form you cannot see in mirrors.

2.15 BLANK BALE DRILL

Purpose

Removing the distraction of the flight of the arrows and their landing points on a target face allows you to concentrate on how your shot feels and what your rhythm is like; you will eventually memorize these aspects so they will become managed subconsciously while your conscious mind is consumed with aiming.

Signs It Is Needed

If your shot seems too variable or needs to be tightened up, this is the drill for you.

How to Do It

Blank bale shooting is shooting at an archery butt that has no target face on it, usually at very close distance (two or three paces). Because you are so close, you must be careful to move your arrow hits around the whole face of the butt so you do not accidentally damage arrows in the butt with later shots.

Pick a shot element you want to focus your attention on (e.g., your release). Shoot arrows in succession, focusing on what you want to happen and identifying how that performance feels. You must focus intensely; do not let your mind wander. After 10 to 15 minutes, you can switch to another form element you wish to work on. Work on only one thing at a time, though.

Tips

If you are practicing for indoor shooting, you can place the butt at shoulder level. If practicing for longer shots outdoors, place the butt somewhat higher so as to adopt the angle your body will typically be at full draw.

Some people stick two-inch- or three-inch-round (5-7 cm) colored stickers all over the butt to aim at, eliminating the possibility of damaging arrows already in the butt.

If you have very limited training time and can set up to shoot at your home, you will reduce not only walking time back and forth to the target but also travel time back and forth to your archery practice range.

2.16 BLIND BALE DRILL (COMPOUND)

Purpose

By removing the distraction of vision, the blind bale drill allows you to concentrate on how your release aid trips and what your rhythm is like; you will eventually memorize these aspects so they will become managed subconsciously while your conscious mind is consumed with aiming.

Signs It Is Needed

If your shot seems too variable or needs to be tightened up, this is the drill for you.

How to Do It

Blind bale shooting is blank bale shooting done with your eyes closed. Usually you make sure any shot will land on the butt before closing your eyes (for safety). Because you are so close, you must be careful to move your arrow hits around the whole face of the butt so you do not accidentally damage arrows in the butt with later shots.

Pick a shot element you want to focus your attention on (e.g., your release). Shoot arrows in succession, focusing on what you want to happen and identifying how that performance feels. You must focus intensely; do not let your mind wander. After 10 to 15 minutes, you can switch to another form element you wish to work on. Work on only one thing at a time, though.

Tips

If you are practicing for indoor shooting, you can place the butt at shoulder level. If practicing for longer shots outdoors, place the butt somewhat higher so as to adopt the angle your body will typically be at full draw.

If you have very limited training time and can set up to shoot at your home, you will reduce not only walking time back and forth to the target but also travel time back and forth to your archery practice range.

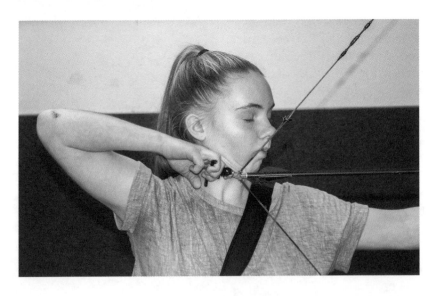

Chapter 3

Flawless Execution

If you look at the books about archery in any bookstore (new or used), you will find that the vast majority are about one topic: how to shoot arrows from a bow. This is unfortunate because it doesn't take very long to acquire that technique. If you practice diligently and frequently, it would take months or even weeks, not years, to achieve good basic archery form to the point that you've "got it."

Of course if you are a serious archer, refining your technique is an ongoing process. But another body of knowledge is bigger and more important than archery technique, and that is archery skill. Acquiring archery skill becomes the focus of most archers' training fairly quickly.

So, what is an archery skill? A simple explanation is that archery skills are what allow you to shoot arrows from your bow into a good—even a winning—score. As an example, say you are shooting on a flat target field and enjoying yourself, but there is a storm brewing and the wind picks up quite a bit. Unlike some other sports, archery competitions are not called off because of wind or rain.

How do you adjust for the wind? There are several techniques, but which works best for you? Do you know? Do you know how using that technique will affect your score? How do you adjust for the rain? Or a flooded field? In field archery, the targets are often at fairly steep angles, uphill and downhill; how do you adjust for that? How do you adjust for shooting when you are tired or mildly ill? The list goes on and on.

Traditionally, archery students were encouraged to enter competitions, and it was assumed the competitions would teach them what they needed to know. This makes no sense whatsoever. Do we leave shooting technique to archers to discover on their own? Do we leave bow tuning to archers to learn on their own? Archery skills can be learned through methods other than through on-the-job training. And you will need to master a great many archery skills if you want to succeed at a high level. The drills offered here provide ideas for what you can do. But it wouldn't hurt to keep your ears peeled for examples of archery difficulties and how archers cope with them.

The best prepared archers succeed the most often. If it rains, prepared archers have their rain gear with them. If a bow malfunctions, they have a backup. If the wind blows, they practiced their wind shooting just days ago. As an exercise, think about all the things that could go wrong and how you could deal with them. Here is just one example: Steve experienced a wave of biting flies in the middle of a competition. The itch from the bites was incredibly distracting. He no longer goes to an outdoor competition without bug repellent spray in his toolbox.

You cannot prepare for everything. American compound archer Dave Cousins got on a plane to Sweden to compete in the World Archery Field Championships. He got there but his bow, arrows, release aids, and other gear did not. He borrowed a teammate's backup bow, some arrows, and a release aid; got the rig together; and tuned during practice. After the first day of competition he was in second place. A performance like that doesn't take technique, it takes skill (and mental strength).

FORM AND EXECUTION

The term *archery form* often includes execution. But in some circles, archery form is referred to as *archery posture*, meaning the body positions an archer moves between while making a shot. If form is limited to the positions we put our bodies into at each stage of a shot, then *archery execution* refers to the movements we make to get from one posture to another.

As a general principle, avoid extraneous motion. For example, raising your bow overhead and then dropping it down into shooting position is a great waste of energy. Why raise it that high if you are only going to lower it? Also, the muscles used to lower the bow work under different conditions than when the bow is raised. Just raising the bow and stopping puts the muscles in a more consistent state of contraction than going up and then coming down. In general, this principle of economic movement applies to every archery move. You want to expend minimal energy to get to each point, at least as a starting point.

You also want to spend the least amount of time possible under great physical stress. For example, drawing very, very slowly may be a great exercise to develop archery muscles, but it is a poor procedure for shooting arrows. The very slow movements consume a great deal of muscle energy, leaving little to execute the rest of the shot (plus fatigued muscles get shaky). Very rapid movements should be avoided as well because they create greater variance in the position of your body at the end of the movement, requiring time to make minor adjustments and to wait for the vigorous movements to die down to a state of stillness.

Another general principle is to distinguish between what you do and what just happens. For example, if using a finger release, do not remove your fingers from the bowstring—that would be doing something. Instead, just stop holding the string. If you do that, the string pushes the relaxed fingers out of the way as it moves back toward the bow. If you try to remove your fingers, they become stiff and impede the string's movement much more.

Here are a number of drills to get you thinking about how to best execute your shots.

3.1 SCORING WITH SIGHTS

Purpose

This drill gives effective practice in scoring well by aiming off and by being focused on scoring.

Signs It Is Needed

If you find your scores faltering under pressure or changing conditions (e.g., weather), you need to bolster your ability to score well under those conditions.

How to Do It

This is a shooting drill limited to those using sights. Deliberately mis-set your sight so that aiming at the center of a target will result in a miss. If you are not sure how much to move your sight's aperture, do it in stages (a little at a time) until your miss is substantial but still on the target face. Then figure out where to aim to hit the target center. Once you figure that out, compare your group size with your groups when your sight is not mis-set. (It should not be greatly different but may be slightly larger.)

Variations

You can deliberately set your sights low or high or left or right of center and any combination of those. After several shots, change your sight's settings and repeat.

Tips

When aiming off-center like this, you can use cue words or phrases, such as "11 o'clock in the black," to help you consistently find your point of aim. Alternatively, you can visualize an aiming dot (in a contrasting color) on the target face at your aim point and aim at that.

MAKE IT A GAME

If you have a shooting partner, mis-set each other's sights. The game is to discover how to aim to score well and then shoot the better score within a set number of shots (three to six).

Imagining an aiming dot on a target face is a good way to memorize a point of aim that is off-center.

3.2 SHOOTING FAST AND SLOW

Purpose

This drill helps you integrate the steps in your shot sequence into a fluid whole and helps identify your natural shot tempo.

Signs It Is Needed

Your shots lack consistency of feel and outcome.

How to Do It

Start by shooting arrows normally until you feel comfortable, then shoot a few more, taking each shot more slowly than the previous one. Attend to the difficulties that arise in your shot. Go back to shooting normally, then shoot a few more arrows, taking each shot more quickly than the previous one. Attend to the difficulties that arise in your shot.

Note the signs that indicate you are shooting too slowly or too quickly.

Tips

If you have a metronome, setting the rate of ticking that seems to match your normal shot allows you to raise or lower your shooting speed more smoothly by adjusting the metronome to click slightly differently in stages.

Purpose

This drill teaches you how to rapidly get on your point of aim, with aperture or arrow point.

Signs It Is Needed

If you feel rushed at full draw, you may be taking more time than is necessary for the preceding steps. This drill will help.

How to Do It

This is a shooting drill best done fairly close up. Get some two-or three-inch (5-7 cm) press-on dots (varied colors work best) and number them 1 to 6. Apply the stickers to a target face in spots quite spread out. After warming up, shoot an arrow, aiming at sticker 1 before shifting your aim to the target center and shooting; then aim at sticker 2 before aiming and shooting at the target center. Then shoot another arrow, centering on sticker 3, then sticker 4, before shooting. Then do 5 and 6 similarly.

Variations

Once you are comfortable with the one-dot sequence, try two-dot sequences: Aim at 1, then 2, then the target center before releasing. Keep adding aiming dots. Go as close to the six aiming points in a row as you can before releasing while keeping good form. Plus, there is no reason you cannot shoot at the aiming dots!

3.4 CALL THE SHOT

Purpose

To compete at a high level, an archer must compare the outcome of each shot with an estimation of how well the shot was performed, usually by reviewing the arrow just shot from memory. This drill helps archers store their shots in short-term memory to recall them so they can compare that with where their arrows actually land on the target.

Signs It Is Needed

Archers who cannot replay a video, including sights and feels, of their previous shot in their minds from memory are at a disadvantage and need to practice this. Archers must be able to recall at least a "snapshot" of where their sight aperture or arrow point was at the moment of release. (Realize that it is moving.)

How to Do It

This is easiest done with a helper. After your arrow is away, turn your head up the line so you can't see the target and tell your helper where the arrow landed. The helper uses a spotting scope or binoculars to check the actual hit point of the arrow and relays that position back to you.

Positions on target faces, at least the round ones, are usually given by overlaying an imaginary old-style clock face on the target face. Positions are indicated by color and time ("Your arrow is at 8:30 in the red") or by scoring ring and time ("It's a 7-ring at 2 o'clock hit").

Variations

If you get bored shooting at the center and hitting it, try aiming off. Aim at 6 o'clock in the red or 11 o'clock in the 4-ring.

If you do not have a helper, you can do this by yourself. Call the shot out loud, then check the position of the arrow with your optics. Some do this while running a video camera. Both the call and the spot are called out to the camera, which makes a running record of the drill results. You can then watch the video by yourself or with your coach and count up how many hits and misses you had in a session.

Tips

Obviously the distance of the target varies with the skill of the archer. If you cannot reliably hit a target where you are aiming, then you need to move the target closer to do this drill. This requires a well-tuned bow and arrow and a skilled archer.

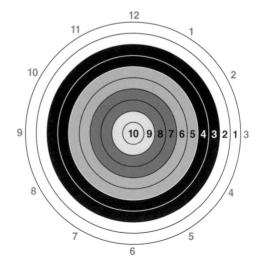

Archers use traditional clock hand positions to identify locations on round targets.

3.5 CHECKING YOUR FOOT-TO-FOOT WEIGHT DISTRIBUTION

Purpose

This drill verifies that you are in balance at full draw and that your weight distribution is good.

Signs It Is Needed

If you are not as steady at full draw as you would like or if an observer (coach, shooting partner) notices that you are balanced more on one leg than the other, this drill will help identify and fix those problems.

How to Do It

You will need a helper and two ordinary bathroom scales (the nondigital kind work best). Weigh yourself on each scale. If the two weights match within 1 or 2 pounds (<1 kg), they are suitable for this drill. (If not, one or both may need adjusting.)

Set up two scales so they will be underfoot while you are in your normal stance. Place one foot on each scale and stand as balanced as you can. Have your helper read the scales. They should read the same weight, within one or two pounds, that weight being half your full weight.

Then have your helper pass you your bow, and you draw and anchor in your best full draw position. Your helper then reads the scales again. Each scale should read half your weight combined with your bow's, again within one or two pounds.

If you are favoring one leg, see if you can get the two readings to match. Your helper can call out readings as they change. Take frequent rests because holding at full draw is strenuous.

When you are in balance, try to remember that feel.

Variations

If you can collect three or four scales you can check front–rear balance as well as left–right balance. You are looking for equal weight distribution or a slightly front-heavy balance point. If you cannot get this many scales, use the two you have and a wooden block (the same height as the scale). Put the toes of one foot on one scale and your heel on the other; place your other foot on the block so you are level. Then read front–back weight distributions under the conditions just described.

Tips

If you have three or four scales, it might help to have multiple helpers to read them.

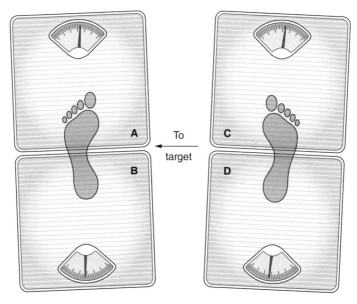

A set of ordinary bathroom scales can help you determine your weight distribution and assist with adjusting it if necessary.

Purpose

This drill makes sure your bow is straight up and down (i.e., plumb) when you shoot. Compound bow archers have bubble levels to help them find plumb, so this is mainly a problem for recurve archers.

Signs It Is Needed

Some archers, especially traditional archers, shoot with the bow canted, which is not a problem if you shoot off the point. But if you shoot with a bow sight, canting the bow throws off all your sight marks if the cant is different from the one used during sighting in.

If an observer (coach, shooting partner) notes that you are canting your bow, you need help getting it plumb. (A variable left–right cant creates variable left–right shots.)

How to Do It

Draw in the vicinity of a vertical upright (e.g., a building's edge, the side of a target hut on a field range, a fence post), and when you have achieved anchor, compare the verticality of the inside edge of your bow's sight window. Let down when done. Repeat as necessary.

Variations

Commercial sight-level tools include a bubble sight you can clamp onto your sight bar. Clamp on such a bubble level, draw, anchor, and then check the bubble. The feedback will help you find plumb more consistently.

Tips

If you find yourself fighting finding plumb, look to your bow's grip. If any of the angles are off, it will make you fight holding the bow plumb. Adjust your grip section as necessary.

A number of companies make bubble levels to clamp onto sights or even bowstrings, or you can make your own level.

Purpose

This drill makes sure your bow is straight up and down (i.e., plumb) when you shoot.

Signs It Is Needed

Some archers, especially traditional archers, shoot with the bow canted, which is not a problem if you shoot off the point. But if you shoot with a bow sight, canting the bow throws off all your sight marks if the cant is different from the one used during sighting in.

If an observer (coach, shooting partner) notes that you are canting your bow, you need help getting it plumb. (A variable left–right cant creates variable left–right shots.)

How to Do It

You will need a helper and an extra bowstring. While you are on the shooting line (shooting at an up-close target butt first for safety), your helper loops the small loop end of the extra bowstring around your top limb tip and then stands behind you. Raise your bow and then anchor. Your assistant will tug your top limb gently left or right to get your bow plumb (by eye). Let down. Repeat as necessary.

Variations

Once you are comfortable with the drill, you can shoot after being corrected to see what having a plumb bow does to your followthrough and arrow groups.

Tips

When you shoot, the extra bowstring may be pulled out of your helper's hands, so after making the corrections, the helper should hold the string very loosely.

3.8 PEEP SIGHT CENTERING

Purpose

This drill builds the important habit of collimating (centering) your peep sight with your aperture. It also helps you set your head position properly.

Signs It Is Needed

Anyone who uses a peep sight needs to develop this skill. If you experience perplexing misses after moving from long to short shots on field courses, this drill will help. (Longer distances loosen up your anchor, and shorter distances tighten your anchor because of the position of the sight block on the sight bar.)

How to Do It

As soon as you come to anchor, the first thing to do is place your sight in the center of the peep sight view. Practice this so you can do it quickly. If you use a scope, it should be easy to align the edge on the scope body with the edges of the peep sight hole. (If you cannot see the entire scope through your peep, adjust things until you can.) When using a pin sight, the goal is to place the sight pin in the center of the peep sight view.

Variations

You can do this drill without shooting. When shooting, you can double or even triple this drill: Proceed up to the point of lining up your aperture in your peep, then let down and start over, then shoot.

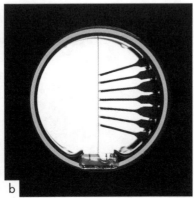

(a) Compound scopes are centered in the peep hole such that a small amount of space can be seen around the round scope body. (b) Pin sights can be a problem because they are harder to place in the center of the peep hole. Many pin sights are now being made with circular housings to aid in this process (they get centered like scopes).

3.9 FACIAL STRING CLEARANCE AND ANCHOR DRILL

Purpose

This drill identifies and eliminates excessive contact of the bowstring with your face at anchor.

Signs It Is Needed

The primary clue this is a problem is excessive horizontal group variation. Contact of the bowstring with any part of your body (especially your face) will expand your horizontal group pattern. The light holding weight of a compound bow exaggerates the effects of excess facial contact.

How to Do It

This drill is very simple. Start off looking into a mirror so you can see the string at your face while at anchor, or have an assistant take digital photos of you shooting. Look closely for contact that causes deformation of your facial features. If your nose is crushed or you can see folds of skin at your chin, then your contact is excessive. Make adjustments until all facial contact is light and gentle and does not distort your facial features. If you are comfortable with strong contact, it will take an effort to get comfortable with light contact.

Variations

Practice maintaining the string in front of your face versus into your face. In other words, keep yourself behind the string by keeping the string in front of you instead of pulling it into you.

Tips

Try being at full draw with zero contact of your face with the string while maintaining peep sight alignment on a compound bow or string alignment on a recurve bow (without a peep). Notice whether your left and right arrow impact points change with zero contact. They should not. If they do, you are likely making too much contact.

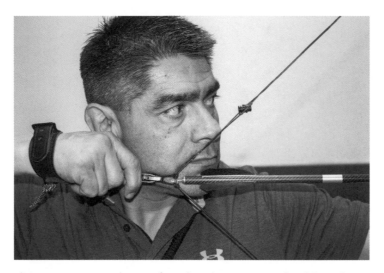

The string can touch your face but the pressure should not be too high.

Purpose

This drill helps you become comfortable with aiming off the center when shooting outdoors in the elements. Having a plan for operating under inclement conditions reduces your uncertainty and increases your ability to adjust quickly and with confidence.

Signs It Is Needed

You struggle to set up and execute your shot when not aiming at the middle. It is natural to aim at the middle; it is not natural trying to find a point away from the center to shoot at. You find that you migrate back to the middle even when wishing to aim off.

How to Do It

This drill is for those who look at the target rather than their aperture as their focus point. If you prefer to focus on your sight, you will need a different drill.

Pick an aiming point that is off-center based on how strong you feel the wind is moving the arrow. Let's say you pick 3 o'clock, 8-ring. Using the target acquisition skills learned in the Aiming on Center drill (see chapter 2), focus in the very beginning of your drawing cycle on 3 o'clock, 8-ring, and keep your eye there the entire time. Avoid second-guessing or making last-second changes. Practice executing a strong, quick, deliberate shot, holding your focus on the chosen aiming point all the way through the followthrough. Exaggerate holding your focus on your original focus point. Adjust your aiming point based on the arrow movement until you are finding the center.

Tips

The key to this method is not to second-guess but to hold your focus on the preselected point. Your body will adjust to changes in the wind force just fine because you have held your focus point.

Repeating the aim point over and over ("3 o'clock, 8-ring . . . 3 o'clock, 8-ring . . .") while aiming can help keep you on that spot, as will imagining an aiming dot (in a contrasting color) at that point.

3.11 AIMING IN THE WIND 2

Purpose

This drill helps you become comfortable with aiming off the center when shooting outdoors in the elements. Having a plan for operating under inclement conditions reduces your uncertainty and increases your ability to adjust quickly and with confidence.

Signs It Is Needed

You struggle to set up and execute your shot when not aiming at the middle. It is natural to aim at the middle; it is not natural trying to find a point away from the center to shoot at. You find that you migrate back to the middle even when wishing to aim off.

How to Do It

This drill is for those who look at the target rather than the pin as their focus point. If you prefer to focus on your sight, you will need a different drill.

First pick the point you will aim at (e.g., 3 o'clock, 8-ring). Start aiming by focusing on the center, but hold your sight off the middle and in your peripheral vision on your point of aim. At the beginning of your shot sequence and pre-draw, keep your focus on the off-center point you picked, and keep it there through your draw cycle. After you have reached full draw and anchor, shift your focus to the middle of the middle, allowing your bow and sight picture to float in your peripheral vision on your off-center location.

Repeat as needed.

Tips

Stay focused through the execution process on the middle of the middle as you would when shooting indoors or without wind. Some archers believe that having the sight aperture only in peripheral vision reduces the anxiety of its movements, allowing smoother execution. The key challenge in this drill is to train yourself to keep your eye on the middle while your sight is not.

Repeating the aim point over and over ("3 o'clock, 8-ring . . . 3 o'clock, 8-ring . . .") while aiming can help keep you on that spot, as will imagining an aiming dot (in a contrasting color) at that point.

Purpose

This drill teaches you that your sight's aperture does not need to be held in the middle to hit the middle.

Signs It Is Needed

You feel you are trying to force your sight's aperture onto the target center and that your aiming ends the instant the release or the clicker goes off.

How to Do It

Start off up close and with a very big target face. The condition you are creating is for the sight pin or dot or loop to be swimming in the spot or center of the target. Take turns aiming in different locations of the giant central spot off-center and on the shot moving or floating toward the center. The idea is to stay loose, relaxed, and mobile. When you lock up, there is very little opportunity to move the shot. If you stay loose, your eye will send the message to your body to make subtle adjustments on the shot without your trying.

If you can do this drill up close on the big target, move back in stages to a correct-sized target. When the target shrinks, it is actually easier to see the results a subtle movement can make.

This drill teaches you that deliberately moving to the middle is not necessary. Without it you would have to execute by holding on the middle all the time. This drill will build the faith that you don't need to be on the middle to hit the middle. It also reinforces the need to keep your eyes involved in the shot and keep aiming after the arrow has gone, up to the point of it hitting the target.

Tips

Do your best to let your eye drive the adjustments instead of consciously trying to jerk the bow onto center. When this is done properly, the motion is fluid and completely subconscious.

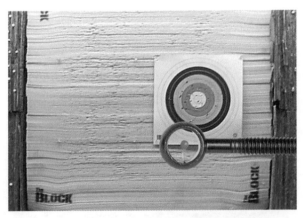

The aiming dot or pin or loop will move subconsciously onto your point of aim if you stay loose. Your aperture will often settle slightly off-center (or off of your point of aim). It will self-center (that is, move to the middle) if you let it.

3.13 DEEP HOOK FINGER GRIP ON THE BOWSTRING

Purpose

This drill creates consistency in placing your fingers on the string. (See the Shallow Hook Finger Grip on the Bowstring drill.)

Signs It Is Needed

If you get unexpected results on a shot you felt was good, varying finger pressures may be the cause. In extreme cases you can pinch the nock end of the arrow enough to miss the target completely.

How to Do It

Perform this shooting drill at no more than 10 paces from the target, with a target face.

Start by placing your fingers on the string, going just past the first crease on the middle finger and at the first crease on the first and third fingers, using the "one over and two under the arrow" string grip. As you draw the bow, focus on creating most of the tension on the middle finger while maintaining the first and third fingers in the first joint. Pay close attention to the separation of your fingers from the nock of the arrow; neither should be pressing on the nock because any contact will cause a deflection in the path of the arrow.

Adjust the starting position by moving your middle finger closer to the arrow and then farther away from the arrow until the ideal clearance is achieved. Focus on relaxing the drawing hand while maintaining the string's position on your fingers. Visually note the starting position of the tab versus the arrow so you can precisely duplicate the exact location of both the tab and your fingers on every shot.

Tips

The position of your thumb is important and can change the pressures in your drawing hand dramatically. Raising the thumb to the first finger loads the top finger more and raises the draw elbow. Lowering the thumb to the third finger unloads the top finger and loads the second and third more. Any change in finger tension will change the arrow impact point at the target. More top-finger pressure makes you shoot higher, and more on the third finger makes the impact lower.

Using a finger separator on your tab is highly recommended.

(a) With a deep hook, the fingers wrap around the string more. The string is slightly behind the first finger grooves. *(b)* No matter where the tab lies, the fingers must clear the arrow (no contact with the string).

3.14 SHALLOW HOOK FINGER GRIP ON THE BOWSTRING

Purpose

This drill creates consistency in placing your fingers on the string in a shallow finger grip. The benefit of the shallow hook is that your fingers can have less than ideal angles and still clear the arrow. (See the Deep Hook Finger Grip on the Bowstring drill.)

Signs It Is Needed

You struggle to get your fingers to settle on the finger tab and string. You get left and right shots for unexplained reasons or even high and low shots.

How to Do It

Perform this shooting drill at no more than 10 paces from the target, with a target face.

Start by placing your fingers on the string, with your middle finger at the first joint and index and ring fingers slightly ahead of the first joint. As you draw the string to anchor, your top and bottom fingers will tend to move farther out on the string toward the fingertips. The objective is to load up on the middle finger and place just enough load on the top and bottom so they do not slide or move.

Adjust the position of the fingers around the spacer and tab opening until the desired results occur (complete clearance between the fingers and nock). Because your full draw position is affected by the string angle at full draw, you must move the starting point vertically in order to find the sweet spot.

Tips

The position of your thumb is important and can change the pressures in your drawing hand dramatically. Raising the thumb to the first finger loads the top finger more and raises the draw elbow. Lowering the thumb to the third finger unloads the top finger and loads the second and third more. Any change in finger tension will change the arrow impact point at the target. More top-finger pressure makes you shoot higher, and more on the third finger makes the impact lower.

Using a finger spacer on your tab is still valuable but not as critical as with a deep hook.

With a shallow hook, the fingers wrap around the string less. The string is slightly ahead of the first finger grooves. No matter where the tab lies, the fingers must clear the arrow.

3.15 DEEP HOOK FINGER POSITION FOR HANDHELD RELEASE AIDS

Purpose

This drill creates consistency and accuracy when placing your fingers deeply on your handheld release aid.

Signs It Is Needed

You struggle with your shot timing; one shot goes off too quickly and the next too slowly, or you have a tendency to trigger the release instantly rather than slowly.

How to Do It

Perform this shooting drill at no more than 10 paces from the target, with a target face.

How you grip your release aid is a personal preference. For a deep hook, place the handheld release between the first and second creases of your release fingers. Every release is different and must be set up to fit your hand. The key is to be consistent so that your window of execution timing is as narrow as possible.

The most important aspect of this drill is to relax the drawing hand and arm as much as possible and to move your draw scapula to make the release trigger.

Once you have acquired your sight picture in a shot, allow all the tension to run out of your drawing hand; allow your back muscles to hold the bow force, and use gentle back muscle movement to actuate your release. If you shoot a triggerless release (also called back-tension release), you may need to adjust it to be slow enough or have enough travel. Shoot close up, and adjust the speed of the release until the desired timing is achieved (the release is to trip when you are pulling straight back).

Variations

Adjust the angle of rotation of your drawing hand to find the most natural and powerful position first (see the Finding Your Release Anchor Position drill in chapter 2). Any changes in rotation will likely change your impact slightly, so don't be alarmed if you don't hit the middle of the target.

Tips

If you are trying this for the first time, we recommend having a coach or friend supervise so you can make release aid adjustments and possibly adjust the D-loop or draw length to accommodate changes in your hand position.

While making changes to the speed or travel of the release, have a coach or friend watch to help you get set quickly without undesirable events.

Safety Note

Be extra careful to draw with the sight on the target in the event the release goes off early or at the wrong time. Also, draw on a line slightly to the side of your face until you are comfortable with your new setting.

3.16 SHALLOW HOOK FINGER POSITION FOR HANDHELD RELEASE AIDS

Purpose

This drill creates consistency and accuracy when placing your fingers shallowly on your handheld release aid. Control of that exact moment is the most important consideration when shooting compound and release.

Signs It Is Needed

You struggle to get consistent timing when actuating your release aid.

How to Do It

Perform this shooting drill at no more than 10 paces from the target, with or without a target face.

How you grip your release aid is a personal preference. For a shallow hook, place the handheld release at the first joint of the fingers on the release hand. This position creates an open hand at full draw instead of the deep grip position. The open hand or fingertip method promotes fine motor movements in the hand, which combine with back tension to actuate the release. This method takes a great deal of practice and a precise adjustment of the release travel and speed. The benefit of this method is that the fine movements generated to actuate the release promote good timing.

Tips

With a thumb-style release, the trigger position moves the thumb below the pad. With a triggerless release aid, most of the drawing load is placed on the index finger.

3.17 DRAWING ARM FOLLOWTHROUGH

Purpose

This drill helps you develop a fluid followthrough while taking advantage of full extension.

Signs It Is Needed

Your followthrough is stopping short of full extension. This creeps back into your shot, creating larger groups.

How to Do It

This drill requires two people. Your coach is the best option, but any assistant will do in a pinch. Do it up close and on a blank bale.

Prepare to shoot an arrow as you normally would. As you are coming to anchor with either fingers or release aid, shift your thoughts to your followthrough. Imagine you are going to slow it down and stretch it out. Have your assistant watch a few shots to get an estimate of the ending positions of your bow arm and drawing arm. The assistant will then place their open hand as if to catch the elbow of your drawing arm. The hand should be slightly beyond the ending position viewed previously to make you reach to contact it (apply a gentle stretch to the assistant's hand with your elbow). The assistant adjusts the position of the catching hand farther back and around as you get better at hitting it.

Tips

Keep the motion a slow, fluid extension to the hand of your assistant. If you feel you have to force the movement, you are going too far. For the assistant, it is better to achieve contact too soon than not at all, so go easy. Once the archer gets better at reaching for your hand, their movements will improve.

MY FAVORITE DRILL

Perfect Times Five

TOM DORIGATTI

Tom Dorigatti is a frequent contributor to *Archery Focus* magazine on issues of compound archery. His book, *ProActive Archery*, contains a wealth of information about how to shoot and train for compound competition.

My favorite drill is my blind bale drill described in *ProActive Archery*, chapter 18, "Blind Bale" Practice for More Accurate Shooting, but a similar drill has been included already. Another great drill that is "eyes open," but every bit as challenging is the Perfect Times Five drill.

Purpose

In this drill, you shoot five 60 X 300 scores *in a row* at 10 yards (9 m) on a normal-sized target. It is a confidence builder, creating the ability to be in control of your shot. It favors a quick, smooth shot execution that will perform well in tournaments. Slowing down and being careful results in misses. This drill helps archers learn to relax and not press to be precise.

How to Do It

This is an eyes-open drill, and yes, you sight in. You must shoot five consecutive 60 X 300 scores at 10 yards. If you miss an X, your count starts over. It has to be five in a row without missing the X-ring.

Variations

When you accomplish this feat, the next step is simple—five 60 X 300s in a row *scored inside out* (arrows touching ring lines are scored at the lower ring value rather than the ordinary higher ring value). If you touch the line, it is out and you need to start the consecutive string over. This one is *not* easy! Shooting 300 shots in a row at 10 yards without touching the line on the X-ring? Of course, you don't need to shoot all 300 shots during the same session, which really puts a little extra pressure on the first shot when you are resuming the challenge from a previous session.

This always involves real scoring on a normal-sized target (the National Field Archery Association five-spot indoor target is best).

Tips

You don't have to start at 10 yards (9 m); you can start at 7 yards (6.5 m) or even 20 feet (6 m). The fun is sticking with it and making the goal. And once you accomplish something like this, often other challenges don't seem so daunting.

Purpose

This drill teaches you to hold the same pressure from shot to shot on your bow's back wall. The most important goal and consideration is to be consistent. The amount of pressure you generate is a personal choice. The important task is to generate the same load under pressure in a tournament situation as you do in practice sessions.

Signs It Is Needed

You vary the pressure on the back wall, shooting one shot from the valley and your next hard into the wall. When you are under pressure and stressed, you will tend to pull harder against the wall. When shooting uphill and downhill shots in field archery, it becomes increasingly challenging to control your load on the wall.

How to Do It

To do this drill you need only be deliberate, present, and aware of your use of the wall. We recommend setting the load when you reach anchor and maintaining it. Some archers increase the load on the wall as they finish the shot. It may be easier to be consistent by starting on the heavy side and holding the same pressure through execution. Relax your arms and hands while increasing your back tension. The gradual increase in back tension counters the relaxation of your arms and hands.

Variations

Since the amount of load is a personal preference, take the opportunity in practice sessions to try different amounts of pressure against the wall to find consistency. Also notice how the impact changes at the target with different loads. If a change occurs under pressure, you'll then know where the change in impact is coming from.

Tips

Good eccentric timing and tuning will minimize the impact changes that occur with variations in load. There are numerous discussions on the Internet on the subject. If you have dramatic impact changes, search out articles on *creep tuning*.

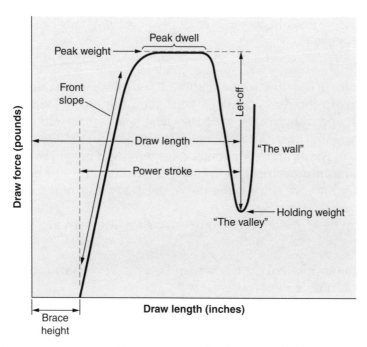

A force-draw curve is created by measuring the force needed at various distances in drawing the bow. A graph is then drawn, filling in all of the points not measured. Various zones and shapes on these curves have been labeled. The wall is the near vertical section at the end of the force-draw curve.

3.19 ABDOMINAL CONTROL

Purpose

This drill facilitates a low center of gravity and improved balance and therefore stillness at full draw. Since the goal is to move the majority of the load of the bow to your core, the best positioning of your core is important.

Signs It Is Needed

Everyone needs this drill. If you notice side-to-side swaying or excessive movement in your sight aperture or arrow point, you may be in an unstable body position.

How to Do It

You can start this drill with or without your bow. As you raise your bow arm and begin the draw phase of your shot, produce a lower abdominal contraction and a slight cave in of the chest. Your spine will curve slightly and flatten out the lower lumbar area of the back. Your pelvis will tilt slightly (from back to front), and your center of gravity will move lower. As you do this, note the improvement in your balance and ability to be steady. The loading of your core helps relax the upper body and make it move more freely to execute your shot.

Once you have mastered this move, try shooting with it.

Variations

Combine the abdominal contraction and pelvic tilt with your breath control to make it a combination move.

Tips

If you struggle to master this drill, martial artists and meditation students have a wonderful explanation of how to do this and how it affects your balance and mobility. In Japanese, the term used is *hara* and they speak of "hara control." An Internet search for these terms will provide descriptions.

3.20 BREATH CONTROL

Purpose

This drill creates consistent control of your breathing pattern, which can lead to greater calmness and stillness at full draw. Controlling your air supply is one of the most important skills to master. It becomes even more critical when you are under pressure, with an escalated heart rate.

Signs It Is Needed

Everyone needs this drill.

How to Do It

You can practice breath control anywhere and anytime. By practicing your breathing in different settings, notice the effect proper oxygen has on your ability to do the following:

- Think clearly
- Have sharp vision
- Have balance
- Be deliberate
- Be in the moment
- See desired outcomes
- Have clear mental images

While shooting your bow, try these steps:

- Before beginning to draw your bow, imagine the perfect shot.
- As you imagine a perfect shot, take a couple of deep breaths.
- Imagine yourself really liking the shot you are about to perform.
- As you draw your bow, take in a large breath.
- Once you come to anchor, let out roughly half of the breath, holding the other half.
- As you execute the rest of the shot, allow air to trickle out your nose.
- On the followthrough, complete the exhale.

Follow up with another slow, deep breath.

Variations

Try different levels of exhalation of the breath you take in as you draw to find the ideal amount that gives you the best energy and peace.

Tips

Look up *heart-centered breathing* and practice it. Being able to call on this method of breath control anytime you need it has powerful value. You will not be disappointed.

3.21 CORE CONTROL

Purpose

This drill teaches you to start off with and maintain a low center of gravity by keeping a flat back and stabilized core. This is similar to the core training used in martial arts to provide balance.

Signs It Is Needed

Everyone needs this drill. If you have poor balance, you will benefit greatly from this drill.

How to Do It

This drill can be done shooting at any distance. As you load an arrow into your bow and prepare to take a shot, tighten your lower abdomen and feel your muscles scrunch up or compress. It is the opposite of standing tall. The small of your back flattens as you rotate your hips forward and upward (top back, bottom forward). Your chest drops and caves in slightly. As you control your breath, feel your chest drop instead of expanding and arching your back. As you draw your bow, maintain the low center of gravity and tightened lower abdominal muscles. It is as if you are slouching. This position (photo *b*) is more stable than standing tall (photo *a*).

Tips

As you work on controlling your core and reducing your center of gravity, keep your head over your hips. Feel as though your spine and neck are a rod centering your head over your core. When done correctly, this drill gives you improved balance and overall stability.

Reach to the Target

FRANK HALLMAN

Frank Hallman is a talented archer, hunter, and coach with a long history of success. Frank is credited with developing the UNI bushing, a machined aluminum piece installed into the rear of an aluminum or carbon arrow shaft, into which a plastic nock can be pressed. Frank was the head coach of the Datus Archery Club's JOAD team, the Nock-Offs, at the club's inception in 1997. During his time as head coach, numerous Olympic-level shooters, nationally ranked juniors, and junior world team members were among those who benefited from his expertise. Some are professional archers today. Frank and his wife, Judy, were the first husband and wife team to be inducted into the Utah Archery Hall of Fame for their accomplishments in archery.

Purpose

This drill is important for all archers and all styles of shooting. It should be incorporated into each and every shot and can be learned up close on a blank bale or just by shooting a target at any distance. Learning this movement technique keeps the bow arm from collapsing on the shot. This drill can be combined with the Move to the Middle drill in this chapter.

How to Do It

Come to full draw and acquire the target. Next, perform a slight inward motion of the bow shoulder toward the target, with the bow hand moving slightly to the left on a right-handed archer. By perfecting this small movement, you effectively eliminate the ability to move in the wrong direction or collapse on the shot. The movement is without load or push—it is just a gentle rotation and reach to the target at the same time, originating at the bow shoulder. If you have extended your arm as far as it will go, you have gone too far. Getting good at this drill will immediately improve your shot execution for both compound and recurve archers.

3.22 MASTERING YOUR HEAD POSITION

Purpose

This drill emphasizes the role of head and shoulder posture in creating balance and leverage. The majority of issues regarding load in your arms are caused by the position of your head. Compound archers commonly hit the wall on their bows and then accommodate that position in their technique, thus losing leverage as well as creating poor balance. Recurve archers commonly accommodate to their cut arrow length. Since your head is heavy and strongly influenced by gravity, practicing this drill will make it easier for you to find your center and stay there.

Signs It Is Needed

You have difficulty maintaining good balance or have poor leverage or too much of the draw load in your arms. Youth who are still growing need to frequently adjust their form and equipment.

How to Do It

Start off up close to either a mirror or a helper shooting digital photos. Use your bow normally, and observe the photos or reflection of yourself in the mirror. Look for the following:

- Is your head centered between your shoulders when viewed from the side? It is okay to be slightly to the rear of your center line, but to be forward of it will compromise your leverage.
- Is your head centered over your hips? A common fault is to lean forward excessively.
- Does the string appear to split your head down the middle? It needs to in order to keep the string in front of your face.

Once you have found and can reproduce your optimal head position, shoot from that position. And since things tend to drift off, check your head position from time to time.

Variations

Starting with your head centered on your neck, make minor adjustments to move your head behind the center line to find the position that creates maximum leverage. In pictures and in the mirror, this should be so slight that it is difficult to see.

Tips

Try gently moving your head back, keeping it behind the string to help actuate your release aid or make your clicker go off. Moving back is better than moving forward and losing leverage. Moving your head back slightly during shot execution will counter the tendency for your head to move forward.

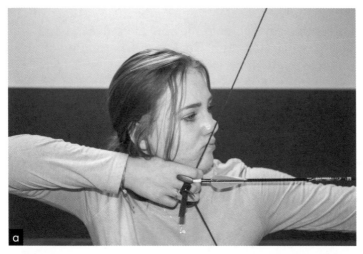

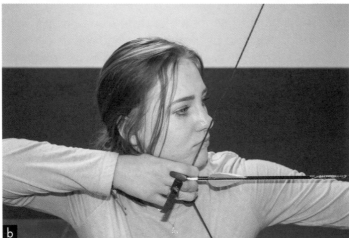

(a) Head position slightly ahead or in front of center.
(b) Head position properly centered with your body.

3.23 STOP SLAPPING YOUR BOW ARM

Purpose

This drill will help you optimize and be consistent in setting the string clearance (also called separation) from your bow arm.

Signs It Is Needed

You sometimes hit your bow arm with the string. Because this drill is so similar to the Bow Shoulder Setting drill (see chapter 2), it is often seen as secondary but should be considered as a supplement to that drill. The element this drill adds is the way you hold the bow in your hand and duplicate that same position as well as the slight clockwise arm rotation of a right-handed archer (counterclockwise for left-handers).

How to Do It

Start on flat ground at a close distance to the target to build the foundation, then move to different distances to develop skill at all bow arm angles. The first part of this drill is setting your hand in your bow consistently. As you rotate your body to full draw, set a visual gap from the bow arm to the string. Practice setting this gap consistently, shot after shot, giving it your full focus. Pay special attention to where your sweet spot is. You will know when you find it. The string will clear and you will feel powerful in your execution of the shot.

Tips

Doing this drill as a brush-up once a month or so will help you accomplish clearance subconsciously and in combination with other parts of your routine. Practice feeling the power when you land in the sweet spot with no arm–string contact. We recommend performing this drill on a blank bale to give it your full attention.

3.24 TRANSFERRING THE LOAD

Purpose

This drill teaches you to unload your arms and shoulders and transfer the force of the bow to your center core, thus moving the load from smaller and weaker muscles to larger, stronger ones.

Signs It Is Needed

Every archer needs to learn how and when to do this. Practicing this valuable skill as a drill will make it an automatic part of your shot process.

How to Do It

Start on flat ground at a close distance to a target. Blank bale is preferable in the development stages of this drill; as you get better, you can choose any distance, with or without a target. (Once you can do this quickly, you need to drive your eye acquisition of the target center sooner.)

As you begin to draw your bow, the smaller muscles in your arms and shoulders become engaged because you are not in position to leverage your back muscles and core. Once at full draw, the load of the bow should move out of your drawing arm and into your back muscles, allowing your drawing arm to unload or relax (the feeling is much like squeezing your shoulder blades together). The bow arm should hold the load set initially until followthrough is complete.

As you come to anchor and your eye has fully acquired the center of the target, move your conscious effort to unloading your drawing hand and forearm by moving the bulk of the load into your back. Focus your attention on relaxing your hand and forearm as the load moves to your back muscles. Hold this relaxed state through the release and followthrough.

Tips

As you improve your skills with this drill, notice how much more fluid your movements are when coming through the clicker or actuating the release aid because of the absence of tension in the drawing arm at the time of execution. Your shot timing often speeds up as a result. As your shot timing speeds up, faster eye acquisition of the target becomes important to not slow down the process.

3.25 GETTING STRING CLEARANCE AT THE CHEST

Purpose

This drill teaches you how to place the bowstring in the same place in relation to your chest from shot to shot.

Signs It Is Needed

If chest clearance varies from shot to shot, you need to correct this. The strength in your bow arm varies from shot to shot because of normal variation. Women should pay special attention to this element because there is most often some amount of contact to control. The string angle on compound bows minimizes the issue, but it is often present with recurve bows. Arm strength is an issue with both bows.

How to Do It

Start off viewing the string on your chest at full draw in a mirror or with digital photos. Draw your bow normally a few times without shooting. Just come to anchor and notice the location of the string at your chest. No contact at all is ideal, but if there is contact, making the contact consistent is important.

For female archers, it is important that the string stay to the outside of your breast, pulled into the side rather than across the face of it. This allows the string to leave in a straight path. If the string is dragging across the breast, it is much more challenging to control the contact pattern (and can result in painful tweaks).

Clearance is controlled by setting the bow shoulder with a consistent gap to the string every time. In addition, by dropping your chest and contracting your abdominal muscles, you will create more room for the string and minimize contact.

Check this clearance regularly. Look for consistency.

Variations

Try different positions of the bow shoulder to find the one that gives you the most strength when aiming. Your holding pattern improves when you find a sweet spot. The key is to have the same gap or contact from shot to shot.

Tips

For recurve bow archers, stopping the draw at the bow shoulder to set this gap helps while you are in the learning stage of controlling the gap. Then a slow draw to anchor will hold the position.

Freezing the Sight Picture off the Center

ED ELIASON

Ed Eliason is one of the most decorated recurve archers on the planet. He has been an Olympic and world team member representing the United States and has won multiple national championships. He is in both the Utah Archery Hall of Fame and the Utah Sports Hall of Fame. He is the only archer in the Utah Sports Hall of Fame.

Purpose

The goal is to place your pin in the center of the target, not as a final act but as an act leading up to the final act. Diligently performing this drill will improve your timing and overall shot execution by locking you on the middle at the time of the shot. The key is to find the middle with your sight pin ahead of locking in your anchor. By doing this, your execution will improve in both shot timing and body control. Archers struggle with this issue for no apparent reason. Ed believes we learn the right way as easily as the wrong way, and so this drill will replace the wrong way with the right way.

How to Do It

Put up a target at close range. Ed believes the habit of freezing off the center comes from locking in at full draw off the center—that is, as you come to full draw, you tend to lock in your form once completing your anchor. In Ed's method, you don't lock in your anchor until you have found the middle with your sight. In that way you lock in on the middle rather than off the middle and then don't have to wrestle the bow to aim it at the middle.

Variations

If you are struggling to perform this drill with your eyes open, close your eyes as you finalize your anchor to build faith in the final movements and to create focus on the final movements without the distraction of aiming.

3.26 FINAL FOLLOWTHROUGH POSITION

Purpose

This drill teaches you to reach past the initial movement of the release and to continue positive movement through the completion of the shot.

Signs It Is Needed

Many archers have a general tendency to stop short or give up on the followthrough. This results in poor groups and scores.

How to Do It

This drill requires an assistant (a coach or friend). Do this drill up close and on a blank bale until you master it. Then you can start using a target at a distance. Starting on the drawing side, have your assistant place their hand in the desired finishing location for the draw elbow. Then you slowly, smoothly, and deliberately continue your followthrough to make contact with your assistant's hand, signaling that you have reached the proper extension on your followthrough. Once you can recognize what this feels like, practice the motion, being as smooth and fluid as you can.

Next, have your assistant move to the bow arm side. The assistant positions their hand forward and four to six inches (10-15 cm) to the outside (to the left on a right-handed archer) of your full draw bow hand position. Practice extending your bow arm to make contact with your assistant's hand as you follow through. Do it slowly, smoothly, and fluidly. As you develop this important skill, you will notice the motion becomes easier to achieve.

Variations

Have the assistant place their hand very close to yours, and you attempt to move the hand with your followthrough in the desired direction until they signal that you have pushed their hand far enough.

Tips

Once you move to a target face, focus on keeping your eye on the middle the entire time you are following through. This is a great aid for aiming as well as for getting the smooth and fluid extension on followthrough you desire. Eye control and full extension complement each other.

The positions of the hands in the followthrough are consequences of the forces at full draw position (the bow is pulling your hands together; the release stops that pull, and your hands should naturally fly apart). You are not trying to create new movements to achieve the described positions; you are trying to stop preventing those motions.

Alphabet Target

RANDI SMITH

Randi Smith has been national para head coach for USA Archery from 2005 through 2018. She has coached archers to five Paralympic medals, including two gold. A level 5 NTS coach, she and her husband, Larry, own Salt Lake Archery. Smith has two master's degrees: one in educational psychology and the other in adapted physical education, both from the University of Utah. She is a licensed professional counselor and therapeutic recreation specialist.

One of my favorite drills is the Alphabet Target drill, which uses an alphabet target we purchased years ago. I don't know if they are still available, but they could be easily drawn on poster board. I allow binoculars or scopes if all teams have access to them. The archers can then spot for each other, and they have to decide who is going for which letters.

Purpose

This drill definitely helps with aiming skills (and maybe spelling?). When it is used as a team event, it can also help archers learn how to work together and get to know one another.

And it is great fun!

How to Do It

Individually. I give the archers a word or phrase, and we see how many ends it takes to get all the letters. I can make it seasonal (Merry Christmas) or archery related (think about process). It's easiest to have them write it out, then cross out the letters as they get them. The difficulty can be tailored to the group.

Teams. I try to have three or four archers to a team (three seems to be the ideal number). I try to make the teams as even in ability as possible by making sure all the top archers are not in the same group. They each get three arrows; for a team of three, that would be a total of nine arrows. I give them a word (six or seven letters), and they try to spell the word. As they get the letters, they leave those arrows in the target.

Variations

For both, the difficulty can be adjusted to the group. With the target, the difficulty can also be adjusted by requiring that the arrow be in the circle or that it can't touch a line.

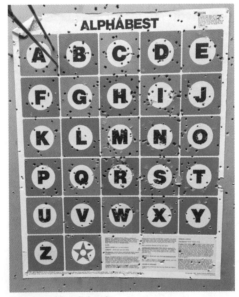

Courtesy of Randi Smith

Chapter 4

Timing and Rhythm

A major part of archery execution is the timing or rhythm with which you make your shots. Since archery is a repetition sport, if you shoot a good shot, you want to shoot another one. A major part of being consistent is shooting in tempo (i.e., with each shot and each element of each shot taking about the same time).

It is claimed that all archers have their own tempo. Although this hasn't been proven, it does seem that way. A key to being consistently successful is discovering your tempo and figuring out how to shoot at that tempo every time you shoot for score. You can quickly prove to yourself that shooting much quicker or much slower than you normally do results in poorer scores. What you are looking for is the sweet spot between shooting too slowly and too quickly, *whatever that means for you.*

Archery is a "feel" sport. If you shoot too quickly or too slowly, you throw all the sensations off. You know this intuitively, but scientific studies also show this. Expert archers always shoot at or near the same tempo, even though they can rush a shot if time is running out (they actually practice doing this). Archers with very fast shots are often picked to anchor team events because if the team uses too much time before getting to the last archer, the speedy archer is more comfortable shooting quickly.

This chapter provides some options to help you find the right timing for your shot and develop your own rhythm. Once you have found a rhythm that is comfortable and provides good results, you can continue to use these drills to refine and tweak your rhythm for continued success.

Purpose

This drill helps you identify your optimal shooting tempo and practice it.

Signs It Is Needed

If you find your shooting tempo is affected by those around you (you shoot slowly when others are slow and quickly when others are quick), you need to learn to control your own tempo. If your shooting tempo is lost from time to time, this drill is a way to get it back.

How to Do It

This drill requires a metronome. Shoot until you are warmed up and shooting with good tempo. Turn the metronome on, and let it run in the background. If you feel rushed or slowed by the pace of the ticking, adjust the metronome. Find the rate of ticking that matches your best shot tempo. Practice shooting at that tempo to the clicking of the metronome in the background.

Tips

Some archers find that a song has the tempo that matches their best shooting tempo. Either recalling the metronome's ticking or recalling that snippet of song can help recover a tempo that is drifting off of optimal.

> ### MAKE IT A GAME
>
> Once you have established your normal tempo, you can make a game out of it by having your coach or shooting partner set the metronome for you (first to a couple of other tempos to confuse your ear, then back to one near your optimal tempo but higher or lower). Shoot several arrows at this tempo, and then tell your helper whether the tempo was too fast or too slow. To make it more difficult, you can also try to state by how many settings it is too high or too low. Take turns with a shooting partner to see who can do it better.

Purpose

This drill allows you to identify your personal shooting tempo.

Signs It Is Needed

If you find your shooting tempo is affected by those around you (you shoot slowly when others are slow and quickly when others are quick), you need to learn to control your own tempo.

How to Do It

You will need a helper for this shooting drill. After you have warmed up and are shooting normally, have your helper time a series of 10 to 12 shots (timing from the moment the stabilizer tip, or any other part of the bow, moves upward to when the shot is loosed works well). After each shot, tell the helper whether the shot felt too slow, too quick, or just right. Repeat until you have made a sizable pool of shots (20-30).

Look to see whether you can identify a pattern: What are the average times for the "too slow" shots, for the "too quick" shots, and for the "just right" shots? Do these make sense? If the perfect shots all went off between 7 and 10 seconds, for example, what should you do? (See the third Putting Your Shot on a Stopwatch drill.)

4.3 PUTTING YOUR SHOT ON A STOPWATCH 2

Purpose

This drill allows you to identify your optimal shooting tempo.

Signs It Is Needed

If you find your shooting tempo is affected by those around you (you shoot slowly when others are slow and quickly when others are quick), you need to learn to control your own tempo.

How to Do It

You will need a helper for this shooting drill. Set up a multi-spot target at a distance you can comfortably score well. After you have warmed up and are shooting normally, have your helper time a series of 10 to 12 shots (timing from the moment the stabilizer tip, or any other part of the bow, moves upward to when the shot is loosed works well). Shoot the spots on the target in order, so that the scores on the shots can be linked to the times of the shots. Repeat until you have a sizable pool of shots (40-60).

Look to see if you can identify a pattern: What are the average times for the high-scoring shots? Do these make sense? If the perfect shots all went off between 6 and 10 seconds, for example, what should you do (see the third Putting Your Shot on a Stopwatch drill)?

MAKE IT A GAME

After you have determined your time slot to shoot in (between too fast and too slow), have a contest with your shooting partner to see who can shoot the most arrows, out of a set of 10 shots, in the correct tempo range. One shoots and the other runs the stopwatch. The count is not shared until the contest is over.

4.4 PUTTING YOUR SHOT ON A STOPWATCH 3

Purpose

Once you have identified your best shooting tempo, this drill allows you to always shoot in your optimal shooting tempo.

Signs It Is Needed

If you find your shooting tempo is affected by those around you (you shoot slowly when others are slow and quickly when others are quick), you need to learn to control your own tempo.

How to Do It

You will need a helper for this shooting drill. Set up a multi-spot target at a distance you can comfortably score well. After you have warmed up and are shooting normally, have your helper time your shots (timing from the moment the stabilizer tip, or any other part of the bow, moves upward to when the shot is loosed works well). If the shot extends to the end of the time for your optimal results, the helper tells you to let down. You must let down.

If your shot goes off too quickly, your helper tells you, "Too quick." Your focus is on getting shots off in good order in the correct tempo. Continue for several ends.

Tips

Archers who have identified their optimal tempo sometimes use a snippet of a song that seems to resonate with that tempo. If they feel their tempo is drifting off while shooting, they will sing or hum this snippet *to themselves* as they shoot a few arrows to recover their good tempo.

MY FAVORITE DRILL

Timed Practice at Blank Bale

LARRY WISE

Larry Wise is a former world field champion who is now a level 5 NTS coach. He has written some of the best-selling books in archery, including his book on compound form and execution, *Core Archery*. He also writes extensively for various magazines. Together with Linda Beck, he developed the Compound National Training System for USA Archery.

This is a drill we often prescribe for members of the Compound Junior Dream Team (a developmental team of USA Archery). It is designed to improve the archer's comfort level and consistency of shot execution within a time constraint.

Set up for blank bale shooting. Then, with the help of a timer, shoot five six-arrow ends (not scored). Each arrow is allotted 20 seconds to shoot, with 20 seconds between shots. On each shot, the main focus is on back muscle loading and contraction while expanding.

This drill can be expanded into a shooting drill at a competitive distance by adding a target face, now shooting six six-arrow ends for score (360 points maximum). Each arrow is allotted 20 seconds to shoot, with 20 seconds between shots.

4.5 COUNTING IT OFF

Purpose

Once you have identified your best shooting tempo, this drill allows you to recover your rhythm if you lose it. The drill should be used only to recover lost tempo, for just a few shots before going back to your ordinary shot process.

Signs It Is Needed

If you lose your shooting tempo from time to time, this drill is a way to get it back.

How to Do It

This is a shooting drill. Set up a butt rather close up (five paces). Shoot until you feel you have established a good rhythm. Then, when you begin to raise your bow, count off until the shot is loosed: 1-2-3-4-5-6-7-8, just like in dance. Try to end on 8 (or 9, or something close—you want enough numbers that the difference between them is small but not so many that the difference is negligible). Once you have a number in mind, shoot blind bale (eyes closed, short distance, no target face) using this count.

"6 . . . 7 . . ."

Variations

Once you are comfortable using this count, shoot at a target face using the count. Try to loose the shot on the count chosen (e.g., 8 or 9 or whatever).

Tips

Compound archers shooting with release aids often take more time at full draw for their release aids to trip. If you work at it, you can get a regular release on your count. It might take more time than for recurve archers.

Chapter 5

Strength and Stamina

If you visit a gym to seek out advice for a weight training program, they will ask you whether you are seeking speed, strength, or power. Archers always answer "strength." If your general physical condition isn't all that good, a strength program will help your archery (and support generally better health). The best exercise for a sport is the sport itself, so this chapter contains archery-related drills that build archery strength using normal archery gear.

If you have access to a gym, you can use those facilities to help build your strength and endurance. When designing a workout program, consult a professional trainer (most fitness clubs employ them), explain what you are doing, and get help designing your program. If no gym is available, there are many archer-based programs posted on the Internet. A search will identify one you can try.

A goal of all target archers is to be able to shoot their last arrow the same way they shot their first. If your muscles get fatigued, you will shake, and in shaking you will not be still, which makes aiming more difficult. Similarly, you will not be able to hold the bow up and the string back as long, so your shot timing is affected. Strength is needed to hold up your bow and to pull the string back. Stamina is needed to ensure you have the time necessary to shoot good shots. If you run out of strength, you will struggle to draw your bow. If your stamina is lacking, as a tournament rolls on your shot will get quicker and quicker because you will run out of energy more quickly with each shot. Both of these effects throw off the feel of your shot, making high-level consistency impossible.

The best drills always mimic what you are doing in the sport, so many of these drills simulate your bow with gym equipment. The key to making these drills effective is to correctly use the muscles (i.e., in the same manner as when you are shooting). This is a basic tenet of any strength training program.

Many a young or beginning archer has claimed, "I can pull that bow," and then twisted themselves into a pretzel shape to draw the bow just once. We then ask them to "draw it again" . . . and again . . . until they fail to pull the string back. (This usually takes only two or three tries. Then we give them a bow they can actually handle.) Having the strength to draw your bow comfortably is important, and so is stamina. These generally develop from longer shooting sessions and over time, but a few drills can really help.

Although some archers believe strongly in training aids, we are unaware of any real evidence that they are effective. However, we have included drills that use training aids to ensure a complete and comprehensive resource.

5.1 DRILLING WITH HEAVIER BOWS

Purpose

Practicing with a heavier drawing bow will develop the muscle strength needed to increase the draw weight of your regular bow.

Safety Note

You can injure yourself if you attempt too much draw weight. You need to be able to draw the heavier bow just like your ordinary bow: level and without distortions of form. If you cannot do this, do not use that bow.

Signs It Is Needed

If you struggle to make distance, one of the factors is draw weight. A higher draw weight will give you a flatter trajectory and therefore a greater cast.

How to Do It

You will need a heavier drawing bow to drill with. For a recurve bow, this can be achieved by using heavier limbs than you are used to. Drills such as Reversals (chapter 1) and Double Draws (chapter 1) will therefore be more effective in increasing your ability to draw your bow.

Tips

If you do not have a heavier bow or heavier limbs, you can add resistance to your bow by attaching rubber stretch bands. A stretch band looped around the bow and your draw elbow can significantly increase the draw force needed to draw that bow.

Purpose

This drill builds strength and endurance as well as understanding of an archer's shot sequence.

Signs It Is Needed

If you fatigue during a competition or practice, then you need to build archery strength and endurance.

How to Do It

Standing in front of a blank butt and close in (for safety), work through your entire shot sequence, taking one whole minute for a single shot. Focus on doing every shot element correctly. Some elements will take less time than others (e.g., the bow reaction is governed more by physics than your body positions).

Tips

If you are using a compound bow, getting from brace to peak weight may be a bit of a struggle because the force-draw curve is so steep; you may need to take less time during that phase. Also, it helps to have a visible clock or timer to see your one minute passing. If this drill is too difficult at first, start with a time you can handle (e.g., 20 seconds) or use a much lower drawing bow. Increase the time, draw weight, or both as you master the drill.

Variations

If this drill proves easy or becomes easy, add time: Make it a minute and a half or two minutes.

Slowly, slowly, slowly . . .

MY FAVORITE DRILL

Holding Your Aim

JOEL MORENO

Joel Moreno is a pro who works with youngsters almost daily. His students benefit from both his talent and passion for the sport. He has a great understanding of the discipline and commitment it takes to succeed, and he manages to instill a great work ethic in his students. This drill is one of his personal favorites.

Purpose

This is an aiming drill that will benefit your accuracy and precision.

Signs It Is Needed

This drill, appropriate for any shooter who uses a sight for aiming, will help develop the ability to stay centered while executing the shot.

How to Do It

To start off, position yourself where you normally would in front of the target. Don't stand too far away—over a long distance, you have to elevate the bow to shoot, and this drill requires you to aim directly at the target. Even though this drill does not include shooting the arrow, it is good to nock an arrow to simulate a shot.

Draw your bow and aim directly at the center of the target. Hold this aiming position for as long as you can. Once you are ready, bring the bow down and relax without releasing the arrow. Repeat this as many times as you feel comfortable, then move back a few steps and start again.

Variations

Windy conditions often force athletes to aim off, either to compensate for a strong gust or after they have moved their sight and then the wind stops. It's literally just pointing the sight or scope at a point that is not the middle of the target.

5.3 DOUBLE DRAWS (TRIPLE, TOO!)

Purpose

This drill doubles the load on the muscles you are using to draw the bow. It does this not by increasing the draw weight but by increasing the number of times you draw your bow.

Signs It Is Needed

If you find yourself feeling stressed at full draw or shaking while shooting, you may need to build up your strength or stamina. If you experience the signs of stress only after you have shot several dozen arrows, then your stamina is in question. If the signs show up immediately, then strength is the issue.

How to Do It

Until you are adept at this drill, place your target butt at just a few paces so you basically cannot miss it. You do not need a target face.

Set up to shoot normally, but after you draw your bow fully, let down but be sure to maintain a couple of inches of draw (less for compound). Then draw again, anchor, and finish the shot.

Start by doing small numbers of repetitions (three to six shots) in small sets (one to three sets of shots). Rest between sets. As you feel more comfortable, you can increase the number of shots in a set and the number of sets.

Warning: There is no surer way to undermine learning than to use a bow that is too stout for you. This is called "being overbowed." If you feel stressed right at the start of shooting, you need to adjust your draw weight downward or swap out your bow for a lighter drawing one.

Variations

Once you have gotten comfortable doing double draws, you can move up to triple draws, which incorporates three draws per shot. You can also increase the load by looping a stretch tube or band around your bow and drawing elbow to increase the effective draw weight of your bow. Start with a light band if trying this until you get used to it.

MAKE IT A GAME

If you have a training partner, you can have contests of 10 shots at a target using double draws to see who gets the better score. Shoot for a prize, maybe a sports drink. Start these competitions at shorter distances until you develop skill. If one of you is a better shot than the other, it is traditional to negotiate a handicap, a number of points to be spotted to the weaker shot.

Tips

This same approach can be applied to many other parts of your shot. For example, you can take your stance, then step off the line and take it again before finishing the shot.

Purpose

This drill builds up stamina and strength around drawing and holding your bow at full draw. This common drill is used to build up to a bow of more draw weight than you are currently shooting.

Signs It Is Needed

If you find yourself feeling stressed at full draw or shaking unnaturally, you may need to build up your strength or stamina. If you experience the signs of stress only after you have shot several dozen arrows, then your stamina is in question. If the signs show up immediately, then strength is the issue.

How to Do It

This drill can be done off a range. Proceed through your shot sequence as normal, but upon reaching anchor, begin to count: 1,001, 1,002, 1,003, and so on. You must maintain good full draw position the entire time you are at full draw. If your form degrades, let down and start over.

Start by doing small numbers of repetitions (three to six holds) in small sets (one to three), with the holds whatever you can manage in length: three seconds, five seconds, and so on. As you feel more comfortable, increase the number of seconds and the number of holds. Elite archers can get up as high as 30 seconds in their sets, but save that for when you are an elite archer.

Tips

You might want to do this drill at the end of a training session so the fatigue it causes won't limit what else you can get done in your session. Also, since you will already be somewhat fatigued at the end of the session, it will make this drill that much more effective.

Do not shoot at the end of a reversal. The fatigue associated with the drill results in unsafe launches of arrows.

Holding . . . 1,001, 1,002, 1,003 . . .

5.5 CLICKER CHECKS FOR STRENGTH AND ENDURANCE

Purpose

This drill for recurve archers builds strength and endurance and helps you be still at full draw.

Signs It Is Needed

If you shake or your sight aperture makes large movements at full draw, you need additional strength or endurance: strength if it happens all the time, endurance if it happens only when you get tired.

How to Do It

Typically you perform clicker checks separated by 30 seconds of rest. A clicker check is done by setting up and drawing normally (have an arrow on the bow and a butt to receive it for safety). Once the clicker clicks, continue to expand for three to five seconds, then let down. A set is three to five repetitions.

Variations

Start with short expansion times and then lengthen them. Start with three reps and progress to five. Start with one set and progress to three.

Tips

Typically during a clicker check, the arrow tip can get only a quarter inch (6 mm) past the clicker blade. If you can get farther past the rear edge of the clicker blade while using good form, you probably need to move your clicker in.

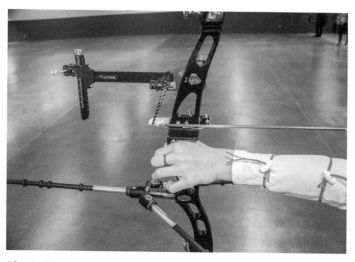

"3, 4, 5 . . ."

MY FAVORITE DRILL

Compression Practice

SIMON NEEDHAM

Simon Needham was an Olympic archer for the United Kingdom and is now a well-respected coach in his native Scotland. He has written two books on Olympic recurve archery, *The Art of Repetition* and *The Competitive Archer*.

My favourite drill is Compression Practice, which involves shooting 10-arrow ends, three minutes per end, for two hours at 70 meters. I used this drill to great effect, and it benefits all archers (compound and recurve) and coaches alike.

This drill started out as an experiment to test the claim that Korean archers shoot 1,000 arrows a day plus go to school and study. This did not seem plausible, so I considered that if the archer shot for two hours before breakfast, lunch, and dinner, they would have time to study, with perhaps an extra hour of shooting later in the evening. How many arrows could be shot in this time frame?

I introduced this to the British junior squads, for both recurve and compound. For a one-hour practice, initially there were complaints of "rushing shots," "too difficult," "not possible," especially from the compound archers, who said the time was too short.

The practice went ahead, with the archers told to shoot the 10 arrows, or as many as they could manage in the three minutes. Collect and return. After a slow start, they all realised it was not as difficult as they first thought; even the compound archers found the pace kept them from wasting time setting up the shot. The weaker archers had arrows left in their quivers toward the end of the practice. Later on, they said they were very comfortable getting their arrows away in head-to-head competition.

Purpose

For coaches, this drill gives a good indication of the strength of your archers; if they are competition fit, they should easily complete the one-hour drill. It helps minimize wasted time during practice.

How to Do It

The range should be set up with a 120-centimeter target face at 70 meters. During the winter I would set this at 60 meters in our indoor range (because of a low roof), the timer set at three minutes with a 10-second lead-in. I would have at least 12 arrows in my quiver (two for spares). I set the timer and shoot the 10 arrows within the three minutes, then swiftly collect the arrows and shoot again, with no breaks. The full practice would last two hours, and I would shoot 280 to 300 arrows.

Variations

The first time I tried this, I did not use a timer, just got on and shot. I thought that as the time passed my group size might degrade. To my surprise, I found that after getting into the rhythm of the shots, the groups became tighter. Each shot had to be a fluid movement, negating any fussing or overaiming, especially after, on subsequent practices, I introduced a countdown timer to help with the cadence of the shots over the three minutes.

Tips

This is a good practice to use a couple of times a month. If time is short and you want a number of arrows shot as a goal, set the distance to help minimize arrow damage and the target face to ensure a good shot cycle.

5.6 DOUBLE AND TRIPLE ENDS

Purpose

This drill reduces the amount of practice time needed as well as enhances shooting endurance.

Signs It Is Needed

If you have limited practice time and would benefit from more or your shooting endurance is somewhat weak, this drill addresses both of those things.

How to Do It

Set up two or more target faces, or mark two or more sets of arrows. After shooting one end of arrows, rest for 30 seconds and then shoot the next end. Score them separately. *Note:* If you are shooting at 70 meters, this saves 140 meters of walking, therefore making practice time more compact.

Variations

Indoors, place multiple target faces on a butt and shoot them in sequence. Use the scores on each target face to analyze your weaknesses and preferences (e.g., if scores on lower-placed target faces are lower, you need to practice more with lower-placed faces; if you regularly score lower on later target faces, your shooting stamina is in question).

> **MAKE IT A GAME**
>
> If you are struggling with a high–low target face bias indoors, have a contest with yourself. Shoot the top face, then the bottom. If the bottom score doesn't equal or beat the top score, you must shoot only the bottom for the next three ends. If the bottom score wins three times in a row, switch to shooting the bottom first, and then try to beat it at the top.

If you find you have a preference for shooting at a target that is top or bottom on a butt, you should consider this a weakness. Set up some target faces at both high and low positions and shoot at them until you score the same on both.

5.7 BUILDING AND MANAGING ARROW COUNTS

Purpose

This drill helps you manage your arrow counts for optimal practice efficiency.

Signs It Is Needed

If you find yourself having long practice sessions and then being sore afterward for days, you are not managing your arrow counts.

How to Do It

A reasonable practice schedule is easy on day one, moderate on day two, heavy on day three, easy on day four, moderate on day five, heavy on day six, and rest on day seven. This varies the load and intensity and maximizes muscle response (growth). To find out what "heavy" is for you, take a practice day and shoot as many arrows as you can while maintaining good form. Whatever that number is, 80 percent of it equals a heavy practice day. Two-thirds of "heavy" equals "moderate," and one-third of "heavy" equals easy. An elite archer may have numbers like 300, 200, 100 (these numbers may vary when preparing for major events).

Count all arrows shot during practice; whether you are shooting a practice round or tuning arrows, count every shot.

Tips

Do not try to change your counts overnight! If you shot 100 arrows in the drill, and therefore 80 equals a heavy workout for you, don't set a goal of 300 for three months from now. These numbers build slowly over time.

Your numbers aren't sacred. Once you find your optimal practice loads, you can stop counting every time and just go by feel. Make an occasional count in case you drift away. Also, the more you shoot, the more you will be able to shoot. As a rough approximation, "heavy" should be no more than twice the number of arrows you will shoot in a day of competition. For example, when the 144-arrow FITA round was used in the Olympics, a maximum day could be 144 arrows plus 50 or 60 in warm-up, so roughly 200 arrows, and many Olympians did 400 arrows on a heavy practice day leading into the Olympics.

5.8 SHOOTING FAST AND SLOW

Purpose

This drill helps integrate the steps in your shot sequence into a fluid whole and helps identify your natural shot tempo.

Signs It Is Needed

Your shots lack consistency of feel and outcome.

How to Do It

Start by shooting arrows normally until you feel comfortable, then shoot a few more, taking each shot more slowly than the previous one. Attend to the difficulties that arise in your shot. Go back to shooting normally, then shoot a few more arrows, taking each shot more quickly than the previous one. Attend to the difficulties that arise in your shot.

Note the signs that indicate you are shooting too slowly or too quickly.

Tips

If you have a metronome, setting the rate of ticking that seems to match your normal shot allows you to raise or lower your shooting speed more smoothly.

5.9 THE 1,000-ARROW CHALLENGE

Purpose

This is the drill to end all drills. After you have done this, nothing will seem difficult ever again.

Signs It Is Needed

If you have reached strong arrow counts in training but still question your abilities, this drill will grant confidence that you can do almost anything you set your mind to.

How to Do It

For most archers, we do not recommend this challenge as stated. Unless you are extremely fit, you can injure yourself or distort your form. Instead, we suggest you set a different goal (see the variations).

You will need a helper or, better, several of them, and a quiver full of arrows, say 10. Set up to shoot blank bale. Shoot the whole quiver, focusing on executing your shots to the best of your ability. After you've shot all 10, your helper pulls the arrows and you rest. Then you shoot the 10 again, and again, and again.

Variations

Instead of 1,000 arrows, try for twice what a heavy practice might involve. Consider taking the 200-arrow challenge first, leading to the 300-arrow challenge, and so on. When you reach a point where you can shoot two, three, or four times what a competitive round requires, you will have proof of your archery fitness, with no doubt in your mind.

Tips

The 1,000-arrow challenge can consume all the daylight hours in a summer day. The lesser challenges will also take considerable time, so allow for that. Instead of repeating this drill over and over, if you need a significant increase in your stamina, spending some time with exercise equipment, in a gym or at home, may be more effective.

5.10 THE NEVER-ENDING END DRILL

Purpose

This drill enhances your shooting stamina.

Signs It Is Needed

Your arrow scores fall off during long ends (five or six arrows), or your scores lag as you get deeper into a competition.

How to Do It

You will need a helper, two archery butts, a large number of arrows, and quite a bit of space. Place two butts with multiple targets (five or six spots) at a 90-degree angle to one another and 45 degrees to the shooting line. Shoot half the arrows in your quiver into one butt, and then turn to the other and shoot the other half. While you are shooting at the next butt, your helper is pulling the arrows from the first. The goal is to keep shooting good shots, with no breaks, until you no longer can. Then you rest and repeat the exercise as many times as you can.

> **MAKE IT A GAME**
>
> You can shoot with a partner to see who can hit the most targets in a row.

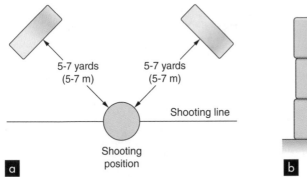

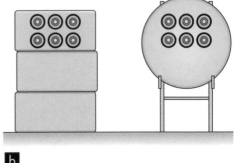

(a) You need a lot of space to do this. Set up one target at just a few paces but at 45 degrees to the target line. Set up another target at 135 degrees from your shooting position. Make sure that shooting on those lines is safe. (b) The target butts need to be high enough to allow for your normal form at competitive distances.

5.11 BASIC DRAWING AND HOLDING (WITH A SHOT TRAINER)

Purpose

This drill ensures that you are using the correct muscles in the later stage of the draw and in the hold.

Signs It Is Needed

If your draw or hold seems shaky, or an observer notices that you are "creeping" at full draw, or if you struggle getting through your clicker, this drill will help create a strong, controlled draw and hold.

How to Do It

After properly fitting your elbow sleeve and adjusting it according to the manufacturer's instructions, without an arrow or even a target butt, prepare to shoot as normal. When you loose, the training aid will keep the string from moving away from your fingers, and if you have not maintained your muscle tension through the shot, it will pull your elbow forward. The goal is to keep this from happening.

It is important to feel yourself pulling with your draw elbow late in the draw cycle. Use the trainer, not your fingers alone.

Variations

You can do this drill with an arrow on the bow, and when the string is loosed, because it moves only an inch or two, the arrow will drop on the floor one to three paces in front of you. If you make a mistake, the arrow can fly much farther, so you should not do this unless you can do it safely.

You can do this drill in front of a target, preferably at the distance you are training for.

Tips

You can perform this drill anywhere as a warm-up for a competition or practice session. It can be done at home as part of your training regimen.

5.12 REVERSALS WITH AN ELBOW SLING TRAINER

Purpose

This drill greatly expands your strength and stamina in drawing your bow.

Signs It Is Needed

If you fatigue early or struggle to draw your bow, you need more strength and stamina.

How to Do It

Adjust the elbow trainer correctly. This drill is just like reversals but with an elbow sling. One full reversal is holding at full draw for X seconds and then relaxing for a number of seconds. A shorter holding time, say 10 or 15 seconds, is advised for those who are new to this drill. When you can do 10 reps at 20 seconds, increase to 25- or 30-second holds.

It is important to feel yourself pulling with your draw elbow late in the draw cycle. Use the trainer, not your fingers alone.

Variations

Take a longer rest period if needed (e.g., a 15-second hold can be followed by a 30-second rest).

If you have a heavier bow or a set of heavier limbs to train with, once you are up to a good number of seconds and a good number of repetitions, say 20-second holds, doing 20 repetitions, switch to the heavier bow. If you can then work up to 20 repetitions with limbs 10 pounds (4.5 kg) heavier than the ones you normally use, then you will never have any difficulty pulling your bow.

"1,016 . . . 1,017 . . . 1,018 . . ."

Chapter 6

Consistency

All the physical training you do has but one end: the development of consistency. The old joke goes, "Shooting a perfect score is easy. There are just two steps. Step 1: Shoot a 10. Step 2: Repeat step 1." This goal of consistency is established in your mind when as a child you shot your first arrows. When you first shoot a bull's-eye, we celebrate with you. When you shoot another, quite some time later, we say, "Good. Now do it again." The goal is to shoot a maximally scoring arrow and then another and another and so on.

Of course, we want to be consistently good, not consistently bad, so consistency isn't a goal in and of itself. But the goal of consistency is the reason we use group size as a measure of archery skill. The ultimate archery group size is the size in which all of an end's arrows will fit into the highest-scoring zone. You cannot score any better than that.

These drills teach you how to measure your consistency and monitor your improvements. Some of the drills bridge you from where you are to an archer who shoots quite tight groups, which allows for ever higher scores.

6.1 BRIDGING

Purpose

This is a drill for better archers, but with modifications of target distance and target size it can be attempted by anyone. It allows you to get comfortable shooting excellent shots over and over.

Signs It Is Needed

This is a tool to build confidence as well as address target panic, so if you lack confidence or have been struggling with target panic, this drill may help (see chapter 9 first).

How to Do It

This drill is typically done indoors. Start with the largest target face available to you at a very short distance (five paces). Shoot five six-arrow ends for a total of 30 arrows. You must shoot five perfect scores for this round. If you miss the center scoring ring, you must start the round over.

After you've shot five perfect scores, move the target face five more paces away. Repeat the shooting process. Move the target face five paces farther away each time you register five perfect scores. When you reach 20 yards (18 m) (three sets of five rounds) and complete the task, move back to five paces and switch to the next smaller-sized target face (if you started with a 122-centimeter face, then 80 centimeters is next).

Repeat until you end up at the full distance with the regulation target face.

Variations

This drill depends greatly on your ability. If you are a highly accurate compound archer, you may want to use the X-ring as a "perfect" shot. If you are a weaker archer, you may want to use the 9-ring. Use whichever ring constitutes an excellent shot for you at this time.

To make the process more difficult, you can force yourself to restart the entire set (rather than just the round) whenever there is a miss. To make it even more difficult, any miss takes you back to the five-pace distance. For massive difficulty, a miss takes you back to five paces and the largest target face.

Tips

It is very easy to lose focus and miss because the targets are so large and so close. Pay attention to what happens with your misses. The key to getting through this drill is focus and relaxation.

MY FAVORITE DRILL

Sight Change

BOB RYDER

Bob Ryder, a national champion and national record setter as a collegiate archer in the United States, became the most successful collegiate archery coach in this country, coaching many championship archers and teams out of James Madison University. He won USA Archery's National Coach of the Year Award and the Maurice Thompson Medal of Honor and is a prolific organizer of competitions.

It's too hard to pick just one drill. But if I have to it would be my Sight Change drill. I can't tell you how many times I have seen good archers lose tournaments because they lost too many points when they changed distances. This is exacerbated because most archers spend all their time practicing the longest distance in preparation for an event. I have my team spend a lot of time at the longest distance but a reasonable amount of time at each distance to be shot.

One point I drive home with my team that has paid off every year in tournaments like this is that if two equal archers are competing in an event with distance changes, the one with the best transitions would win.

With that in mind, I came up with a sight change drill that was invaluable to my team's development. They hated it at first, but once they saw the results they were believers in the system.

It is amazing what a confidence boost each one of the team members gets when their "Tuff FITA Score" (see below for details). matched their personal best. They knew when that happened that they were about to give that personal best a good bump in their next tournament.

When your archers are confident that each first arrow at a new distance will be on the money, they will be tough competitors whether shooting FITA, field, or 3-D competition. It builds a self-confidence that is quite comfortable finding its way to the top of the podium.

Purpose

Teams often need to prepare for FITA rounds or 900 rounds where they need to change distances during an event. This drill is for the FITA round.

How to Do It

1. Make sure all the archers have sight marks for each distance.
2. Set up targets at all distances.
3. Give them two ends of six arrows to warm up (any distance).
4. Announce, "Sight change drill."

5. Have them shoot:

- Two arrows (men at 90 m, women at 70 m)
- One arrow (men at 70 m, women at 60 m)
- Two arrows at 50 m (men and women)
- One arrow at 30 m (men and women)

6. Have them score their ends and note the location of each shot.

7. Have them multiply their scores by 24 to determine their Tuff FITA Score. (A normal FITA round is 1,440 points, so multiplying by 24 gives you a score out of 1,440 points.)

8. Have them go directly to the distance(s) they did poorest at and check the mark for that distance.

Once everyone has had 30 minutes to work out their problems, repeat the drill.

Variations

You can modify this drill for the 900 round by simply shooting two arrows at each of the three distances. You can modify for field or marked 3-D competitions by scrambling the distances and shooting one arrow at each distance.

6.2 SHOOTING FOR GROUPS

Purpose

This is a drill for better archers, but with modifications of target size and distance anyone can attempt it. The drill allows you to get comfortable shooting consistently small groups over and over.

Signs It Is Needed

If your groups are larger than you want or they seem to vary quite a bit from session to session, this drill will establish some parameters that will allow you to track your group sizes.

How to Do It

This is a shooting drill. Start up close and use a multi-spot target. Shoot three arrows at each spot, resting between each three-arrow end. Track your group sizes in one of the following ways:

- *Use decimal scoring.* Break each scoring ring into 10ths and score that way (e.g., an arrow just missing the 9-ring is an 8.9 score); your scoring average is a measure of group sizes.

- *Use the "holding the Y-ring" system.* If all your arrows are within the 9-ring, you are holding the 9-ring, which is an indicator of your group sizes; typically "all" means 95 percent or greater.

- *Measure the perimeter of the group.* Wrap a shoelace around your group and then measure the length of the lace that surrounded your arrows.

Keep records and compare them. Are your groups getting smaller? If not, you aren't getting better.

Do this drill frequently as a way to track your consistency as an archer.

Variations

As you acquire proficiency and better consistency, move to longer distances, always shooting standard-sized target faces.

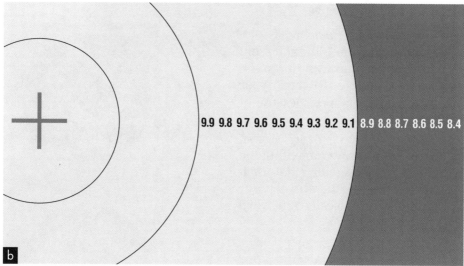

9.9 9.8 9.7 9.6 9.5 9.4 9.3 9.2 9.1 8.9 8.8 8.7 8.6 8.5 8.4

One way of keeping track of how tight your groups are is to use *metric scoring* (also called *Korean scoring*) on your practice rounds. Each arrow is scored to the 10th of the scoring ring value. An arrow just missing the 10-ring would be scored as 9.9, for example. If you score your practice round arrows by the 10th (and your groups are always centered on the target), your score will be an indicator of your group size (higher is better).

6.3 CHECKING YOUR GROUP SIZES

Purpose

This is a drill for better archers, but it can be attempted by anyone. It gives you feedback on your consistency when shooting at various distances.

Signs It Is Needed

If your group sizes are larger than you want or they seem to vary quite a bit from target distance to distance, this drill will establish some parameters that will allow you to track your group sizes, form, and bow tune.

How to Do It

This is an outdoor shooting drill. You will need a large target face at three or more distances, say 20, 40, and 60 yards or meters (these were chosen to make the math more apparent).

Shoot a substantial number of ends (three to five) of six arrows at each distance. Track your group sizes in one of the following ways:

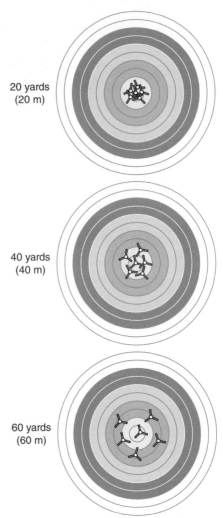

20 yards
(20 m)

40 yards
(40 m)

60 yards
(60 m)

- *Use decimal scoring.* Break each scoring ring into 10ths and score that way (e.g., an arrow just missing the 9-ring is an 8.9 score); your scoring average is a measure of group sizes.

- *Use the "holding the Y-ring" system.* If all your arrows are within the 9-ring, you are holding the 9-ring, which is an indicator of your group sizes; typically "all" is 95 percent or greater.

- *Measure the perimeter of the group.* Wrap a shoelace around your group and then measure the length of material that surrounded your arrows.

The size of your groups should be proportional to the distance shot. So your groups at 40 yards or meters should be two times wider and taller than your groups at 20 yards or meters, and your groups at 60 yards or meters should be three times wider and taller than your groups at 20 and one and a

By shooting the same size target at different distances, you can check your group sizes. At twice the distance, groups should be twice as wide and twice as high. At three times the distance, they should be three times as wide and high.

half times wider and taller than your groups at 40. (If you have odd distances, the group size divided by the distance should be close to the same number.)

If the group sizes are not proportional, your bow or arrows may be out of tune or your form is flawed.

Tips

Take note of your group sizes at each distance. Any arrow shot into such a group size is a normal shot. Too many archers adjust their equipment, mistaking normal shots for abnormal ones, thus making their scoring worse.

6.4 VARYING PRACTICE LOCATIONS

Purpose

This drill helps you adapt to different shooting venues.

Signs It Is Needed

If your scores drop or rise in some locations but not others, this drill will help determine why.

How to Do It

Identify all the shooting halls in your vicinity. Arrange to shoot a practice round at each of the locations, one after another, so that you shoot at all of them once within a short period such as a month or so. Compare the scores with typical scores you shoot at your home practice facility. Take notes. Were there things that bothered you, affecting your scores (lighting, noise, people talking)? Note how you felt: Were you shooting well or were you "off"?

Identify, if possible, the environmental factors that contribute to lower or higher scores. Ideally you want none of the negative factors to affect you. See if you can incorporate any positive effects into your shot.

Tips

If you shoot a multi-spot target face, determine the score on each spot to see if there is a spot bias. Also, control for faces being placed high or low. All faces should be in the same location (high or low) at each of the venues.

MAKE IT A GAME

Pretend you are shooting in a mail-in tournament and that you are going to mail in the sum of the scores from all the venues. Keep the score data. If the drill is useful, repeat it again next year to see if you can better your scores.

Chapter 7

Balance and Stillness

At the moment of truth in archery, the moment just before you loose the bowstring, what you desire is stillness. If you are not still (and you are never perfectly still), you need to contend with holding your bow not only in the correct position in space but also in the correct position in time ("Now . . . no, wait . . . now . . . no, wait . . ."). This makes shooting doubly difficult, so archers work to be still at full draw when aiming so they can focus on the spatial requirements alone. (The actors who shoot while tumbling in the movies [e.g., Legolas, Hawkeye] are shooting arrows pasted in by the movie's computer graphics people.)

Ideally the movement of your sight aperture or arrow point is minimal (they are never perfectly still), with "minimal" defined as not needing conscious correction. The aiming device moves slightly and randomly but inside your desired impact point for your arrow. Excessive movement while aiming results in larger groups (which create lower scores) and can also lead to anxiety, encouraging archers to try to make their bow steadier. Such attempts lead to even more movement and more anxiety. You do not want such negative feedback loops in your shots.

Stillness is affected by balance. If you are out of balance, multiple muscles will engage to move you back into a state of balance, and you *will* move more, whether you want to or not. This task is generally taken care of subconsciously, so you are not very aware of all that happens to balance you. You need to be more aware of this state of stillness and make sure you can create it at full draw in every shot.

If you are a gym fan, the ability to hold still is basically a function of core and leg strength, which should help you choose exercises to work into your conditioning plan in addition to these drills for developing balance and stillness as a part of your shot sequence.

7.1 SHOOTING FROM UNEVEN FOOTING

Purpose

In field archery and even target archery on a rough field, uneven footing is common. This drill allows you to practice shooting where the footing isn't flat. It also improves your sense of balance.

Signs It Is Needed

You are preparing for your first field tournament or for a tournament on a field you have been told has an irregular shooting line.

How to Do It

You will need several pieces of board (short pieces of two-by-four or two-by-six work well), one of which needs to be about three feet (1 m) long. After warming up, place a single board under your target-side foot and shoot a few arrows (simulating uphill footing). Switch the board to your "away" foot (simulating downhill footing). Put the long board against your toes; step up so that your toes are on the board but your heels are still on the ground (this simulates sidehill footing facing into the hill), and then switch so that the board is under your heels, toes still on the ground. Shoot in each orientation to see how your footing affects your steadiness at full draw.

Variations

Double or triple the heights of the boards by stacking them on top of each other.

Tips

If all you have are one-inch-thick boards, stack them to make thicker ones. This drill simulates only footing issues. To get the effects of shooting uphill and downhill, you actually need hills (or simulated hills, such as shooting from your deck in your backyard).

7.2 SHOOTING OFF A BALANCE BOARD

Purpose

This drill creates better balance by requiring you to focus on your balance while shooting.

Signs It Is Needed

If you find yourself swaying at full draw or your sight's aperture displays large movements (very small ones being normal), you need to improve your balance and stillness at full draw.

How to Do It

This is a shooting drill. (Shoot from very close up until you have experience shooting when unbalanced.) You will need a balance board (also called a wobble board), which you can buy or make from scrap materials. A piece of plywood large enough for you to take your stance on, with a small board (one-inch [2.5 cm] square), the same length as the plywood's width, nailed crosswise underneath, will do.

Stand on the wobble board. Draw your bow several times to experience how the board affects your balance, then let down. After you experience the effects, draw and shoot arrows. Focus on executing good shots.

Variations

Replacing the thin board on the bottom with a five-inch circular disk of plywood will create instability in your stance in all directions, not just left–right.

Safety Note

Do not overdo it—the amount of wobble should be very small. If your wobble board allows for too much swaying, shooting from it may be dangerous.

MAKE IT A GAME

If you have a shooting partner, you can hold a contest to see who can shoot the best score from the wobble board.

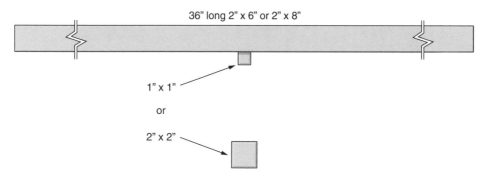

36" long 2" x 6" or 2" x 8"

1" x 1"

or

2" x 2"

Wobble boards (also called *balance boards*) are available commercially but can be made from a two-by-six or two-by-eight piece of scrap lumber, with a one-by-one or two-by-two piece nailed across its center. You take your stance on the board and focus on your balance, shooting arrows without the board toppling all the way to one side or the other.

7.3 SHOOTING OFF OF ONE FOOT

Purpose

This drill creates better balance by requiring you to focus on your balance while shooting.

Signs It Is Needed

If you find yourself swaying at full draw or your sight's aperture displays large movements (very small ones being normal), you need to improve your balance and stillness at full draw.

How to Do It

Start at a close distance before shooting from farther away, for safety. After warming up, try shooting with your feet together (touching). Note any differences in sight picture stability and group size in the target. Then raise one foot off the ground a few inches and again shoot some arrows. Note any differences in sight picture stability and group size in the target. Switch the foot raised and shoot again, noting differences. Then raise both feet off the ground—just kidding!

Tips

Over time you should see improvements in aperture steadiness and group size when doing this drill. You can also explore various stances this way. The best stance is the one that allows you to be the most still and relaxed at full draw.

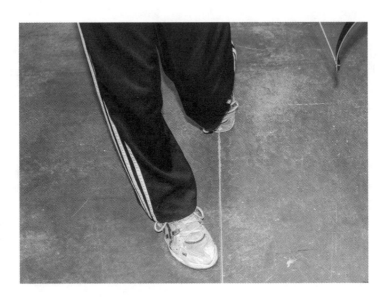

Purpose

Archery puts considerable stress on your neck from turning your head toward the target. This drill stretches the muscles that need to be relaxed to get a good head turn.

Signs It Is Needed

If you have trouble seeing targets around your nose or around eyeglasses, you may need more head turn. In order for you to turn your head *toward* the target more, the muscles responsible for turning your head *away* need to be relaxed. This drill stretches those muscles and allows them to relax.

How to Do It

Either with your bow or a lighter drawing bow, after stretching and warming up, address the target and draw. Once at full draw, turn your head away from the target (over your other shoulder, as it were). Then turn back and let down. If you are at a range, you need to be on the shooting line (i.e., where everyone else is standing) with an arrow on your bow for safety, but do not shoot.

Do not shoot from this position; this is just a stretch to make your normal head turn easier.

7.5 HEAD CANTING

Purpose

This drill educates you with regard to having your head and eyes level. One of the negative effects of a tilted head is poorer balance.

Signs It Is Needed

Canting your head to the left or right causes left and right arrows. If an observer (coach or shooting partner) notices you are tilting your head, this drill will help you correct that.

How to Do It

This drill starts as nonshooting and then transitions to shooting. It is best to start with a light drawing bow quite close to your target.

Draw with your head level and then tilt your head left or right, and then in the opposite direction. Do not overdo it, because you could end up flinging arrows in dangerous positions—you just need a slight tilt. Note the impact of the arrows at the target. If you do not see any difference, try a longer distance.

Tips

Tilting your head up and down has much less effect on your shooting. The goal is eyes level with the ground.

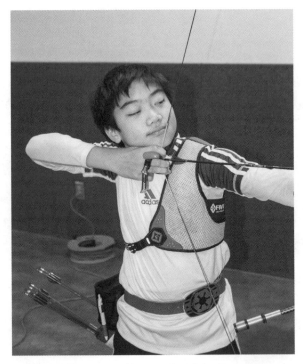

Do not shoot from this position; simply note the distortions that occur with a tipped head.

7.6 EXPLORING BREATHING PATTERNS

Purpose

This drill causes you to examine your breathing to see what breathing pattern works best for you.

Signs It Is Needed

If you find yourself out of breath after a shot on more than very rare occasions, you need to look into a pattern of breathing that better supports your shot.

How to Do It

While shooting arrows, pay attention to your pattern of breaths. Note every inhale and exhale through the entire shot. Write this pattern in your notebook.

If you have been inhaling during the draw, try exhaling during the draw. This may be difficult to do if your normal pattern is ingrained. To exhale during your draw, you must inhale immediately before, so start by inhaling as you raise your bow.

Note how steady you are at full draw and how clean your releases are.

Change the sequence of your breathing, and even change the rate (more slowly, more quickly). Each change will require quite a few shots to feel comfortable and for you to detect whether or not a new breathing pattern is worth investing your training time in.

Tips

Most studies indicate that archers shoot better without full-to-bursting lungs. Many recommend a slight exhale off of an inhale as the best place to hold and shoot from. Try working backward from this state to design a breathing pattern that supports your shot.

If you do find such a breathing pattern, be aware that your breathing is then linked to your shot tempo, and your breathing rate needs to be monitored when you are under competition pressure (when you tend to breathe faster).

Out goes the bad air, and in goes the good.

Chapter 8

Training Mind-Set

Imagine you are shooting well and then something happens and you can't seem to find the skill you were displaying just minutes before. What do you do? If you are unprepared, what could happen is you fail to recover, fall apart, even quit the competition. Being prepared for all eventualities is an aspect of archery that has very little to do with "how to shoot" and everything to do with "how to score well." And we don't mean just changes in wind and weather. Have you considered what you would do if one of the archers in your group was cheating? It is rare but it does happen. In short, any activity that draws your attention away from your shooting will adversely affect your score.

Preparing for competition and the things that can happen in competition includes building the mental skills you incorporate into your shot process. Other aspects include activities outside of shooting, such as planning.

The mental skills that support shooting well include controlling your attention (although you perform subconsciously, you must be present consciously), dealing with interruptions (such as when your equipment breaks or you shoot a poorly scoring arrow for no apparent reason, or someone nearby is accused of cheating), and making sure your subconscious mind knows what task to perform (your subconscious mind tends to flit about, for good reasons—survival, mostly—but this is not good for archery).

This chapter introduces the concepts of the mental game and shows you how to practice them. If you wish to be successful, incorporating a mental program into your practice sessions and competition rounds is the key to getting good results.

Here we offer a number of drills to get you thinking about how to best execute your shots. The mental game of archery constitutes a vast body of knowledge, so we are just trying to get you on the right path. We begin with how to warm up, because starting cold could cause you to shoot poorly early on, which is never a positive.

8.1 JOINT AND MUSCLE ACTIVATION

Purpose

This drill helps archers form a warm-up routine that will activate (i.e., lubricate) the joints involved and prepare the muscles for their roles.

Signs It Is Needed

If your first shots feel awkward or clumsy, but after a few shots your shot flows better, or if you experience joint stiffness or muscle stiffness after shooting, you may need a warm-up routine.

How to Do It

Try the following activities to see whether they help:

- *The pigeon walk.* Bob your head forward and back, similar to what a pigeon does when walking. Repeat as needed.
- *Arm circles.* Stand with both arms straight out to your sides. Rotate the arms so the hands move in about a one-foot (30 cm) circle. Perform 10 rotations in each direction.
- *Arm stretches.* Stand as if shooting, and raise your draw arm up as if reaching for your bow. With your other arm, reach behind your draw elbow and hook your bow arm elbow; pull gently, stretching the muscles used in the early stages of the draw. Switch arms and repeat three to five times.
- *Stretch band mimetics.* Make a loop out of a stretch band or rubber tubing, about half the length of your draw. Loop the band over your bow hand. Execute a draw and loose, with the band standing in for your bow. Repeat as necessary.

Variations

Observe other archers warming up in a similar fashion. Try some of the things they are doing. Make up your own routine of these exercises, and commit to doing them for at least six weeks to see if you benefit from them.

Purpose

This drill keeps you flexible where you need flexibility.

Signs It Is Needed

If you find yourself stiff or sore after a competition, it may be due to a lack of flexibility or unwanted tension while shooting. If you struggle to turn your head far enough to see your target effectively, you have a flexibility problem in your neck.

How to Do It

To turn your head one direction requires that the muscles used to turn your head the other direction be relaxed. If you are suffering pain, those muscles may be tense, inhibiting your head turn. Stretching exercises in which you (always) balance the left and right sides are needed: Turn your head first in one direction, then the other. Focus on relaxing muscles not being used for the turn. Raise your chin to produce a good stretch; lower your chin similarly.

If you have a partner, sit in a chair and have them rotate your head for you . . . gently! Your partner rotates your head in both directions, while you focus entirely on relaxing your neck muscles.

Variations

If other aspects of your shooting create flexibility issues, schedule stretches or drills during your physical training sessions to deal with them in a like fashion.

Tips

Always start easy on these exercises. If you feel sore the next day, that is considered normal. If the soreness extends longer, you may have injured yourself.

When your helper is turning your head for you, make sure you set up a trigger word like "Ow!" that will get them to stop immediately.

Include stretches that address the areas where you experience unwanted tension in your pre-shooting warm-ups.

8.3 STRETCH BAND DRILL

Purpose

This drill allows you to train when you are not at a range or cannot shoot. It will increase your ability to draw your bow.

Signs It Is Needed

If your draw is not smooth and strong, this drill can smooth it out for you while making you stronger.

How to Do It

Make a loop in a rubber stretch band by tying the two ends together. The loop should be about half your draw length. Then, using your best form, draw and release the loop. It should fly out of your hand in a straight line from the draw.

To strengthen your draw, stretch a longer loop around your bow and draw elbow, increasing the resistance of the bow. Drawing the bow or doing reversals (see chapter 1) will build the muscles involved. As always, focus on shooting with your best form and execution.

Tips

When you become proficient in shooting band shots, you can hang onto the band so you won't need to pick it up so often. This drill can be used anywhere you have a small amount of space and time to train.

The stretch band looped over the bow can be turned into a shooting drill when at a range. Focus on finishing the shot against the pull of the stretch band.

8.4 INSTILLING A SHOT SEQUENCE

Purpose

This drill helps infuse your shot with your shot sequence to make it more consistent.

Signs It Is Needed

If under pressure you add steps to, or leave steps out of, your normal shot process, you need this drill. Actually all archers need to know their shot sequence (or shot routine) by heart.

How to Do It

If you do not yet have a shot sequence, you need to create one and write it down prominently in your notebook. This is then a guide for your shot training.

As you shoot arrows, name each shot element as it happens. If you are shooting in public and this makes you self-conscious, you can do it mentally and not out loud. (This allows you to "shout" in your head, which can make this more effective.) Do this for just a few shots, more if you make mistakes.

Variations

Some archers print their sequence on a label and paste it to the top limb and read it before every shot, until it becomes second nature. Other archers carry their sequence on a card in their quivers to consult as needed.

Tips

This is a training drill; you should never consciously work your way through your shot sequence while shooting for score. Shooting needs to be done primarily subconsciously. *Note:* Shot sequences, like shooting techniques, are personal; no two are identical.

> ### MAKE IT A GAME
>
> If you have a shooting partner, have your partner name each element of your shot (working from your list) as you shoot. After several shots you can switch roles. After a few repetitions, put away the lists and do it from memory.

8.5 BUILDING A MENTAL GAME

Purpose

This drill teaches you to keep your attention in the present moment while shooting. Staying in "the now" keeps you busy so there is no time for negatives like fear and doubt to enter into your thinking.

Signs It Is Needed

We all need this one.

How to Do It

Select a mini subroutine in the middle of your shot. Give yourself a starting trigger (*suggestion:* the sound of the nock snapping on the string) and an ending trigger (*suggestion:* the sound of the arrow hitting the target) to define that segment.

During the time in between your shots you can be free to think of whatever comes along, but as soon as you hit your trigger event you must concentrate your efforts on this small window of time and keep your mind busy doing the tasks in your routine, free from outside distractions. If anything other than what you are doing intrudes on your thoughts, you must let down and start over.

This small effort, once built into your normal shot routine, will give you a concentrated and powerful mental game. It forces you to focus without having the majority of your routine clogging your present attention.

8.6 EMPHASIZING SHOT EXECUTION 1

Purpose

This drill teaches you to be completely aware of and in control of your shot execution. In your quest to make the majority of your shot process close to automatic, this is the one aspect of the shot to not take for granted.

Signs It Is Needed

You may feel as though you tune out at the moment of the shot. You feel blank or unaware—the shot just seems to happen. It takes effort to stay present and conscious. The challenge becomes deciding when and where to be conscious versus subconscious. We urge you to keep the execution phase of your shot in the front of conscious attention. This is the one component that the very best archers in the world have command of. Being consciously aware of what is happening keeps your subconscious mind from improvising.

How to Do It

The key is to improve conscious effort and presence at this important moment in your shot. Provide yourself with a positive affirmation and a sound or deliberate movement to actuate a release aid to go off, or to make a clicker go off. Tell yourself before you begin that you are going to like this shot. Tell yourself to enjoy the moment of execution the most of all, but this event will not be the end of the process. You must stay present and in the shot moment well after the arrow has left the bow. You must feel as though you are still guiding the shot even though it is gone and you cannot. Your eyes stay focused on the target and you stay in the shot and most important of all, you enjoy it!

> ### MAKE IT A GAME
>
> Stay in the shot, keeping your eye on the target as long as possible. Time yourself, and push to increase the time window of being in control. Push the level of your control to expand throughout your body to multiple movements at the same time. Enjoy every part of your control and your execution.

8.7 EMPHASIZING SHOT EXECUTION 2

Purpose

This drill emphasizes the most important moment of the shot: the execution just before, during, and after the release.

Signs It Is Needed

The followthroughs of your shots end abruptly. Your eye does not stay focused on the target middle after the arrow is gone. Each shot is over when the release or clicker goes off instead of after the arrow hits the target. Your followthrough and body movement stop too soon.

How to Do It

Start at least 50 paces away from your target. This drill addresses your thought processes by exaggerating your followthrough and body movements. The idea is to slow down, stretch out, and smooth out this very important moment. Use your thoughts and deliberate actions to make the moment a larger window of time. As you actuate your release, focus your energy on executing a smooth, soft body reaction while keeping your eye on the target middle for an extended period. Keep aiming after the shot is well gone. Keep moving your body to the center, and imagine yourself moving in slow motion. Feel fluid. For clicker shooters, tell yourself you are shooting after the click rather than on it. Tell yourself the clicker going off is not the final act—your shot is—so don't rush the moment. Slow it down instead.

Variations

This drill can be customized to your standards. The overall goal is to make this moment deliberate rather than automatic and to allow your eye to stay in the shot and on the target middle longer.

Tips

This control is tougher to hold up close because the arrow is in the target so fast, and that has the ability to cut off your gaze. When the eye stops looking, the body tends to stop. Once you can master this drill, practice up close, keeping your eye engaged even after the arrow hits the target.

Tell yourself that "the shot is not over until the bow takes a (theatrical) bow." Commit to finishing every shot to that point.

Slowly, slowly, slowly . . .

8.8 IMAGERY DRILL

Purpose

This drill incorporates a visualized shot into your shot sequence, making your shot more repeatable and consistent. This is especially helpful after a poorly executed shot.

Signs It Is Needed

Every successful target archer does this (hint, hint). If your shot is not as consistent as you need it to be, this drill will help.

How to Do It

Just before you raise your bow for a shot, visualize a perfect shot (from your viewpoint). See the arrow fly and land in the center of the target face. Imagine all the sounds and scents (everything you can!) associated with such a shot, then raise your bow and execute your shot.

Tips

Commit to this practice. Do it for every shot you take in practice or competition until it is a habit. You can even practice it away from the shooting hall or range. *Note:* The visualization acts as a prescription for what you want your subconscious mind to do. Visualize a miss and you will miss!

Just before you raise your bow, picture a perfect shot as well as you can.

MY FAVORITE DRILL

Self-Talk Practice

LANNY BASSHAM

Lanny Bassham is an Olympic gold-medal-winning rifle shooter who developed an entire mental management system based on his performance at the Olympics, starting with a failure to win gold and ending four years later with his gold medal. His book *With Winning in Mind* is the best-selling mental skills book for the shooting sports.

I wish more shooters were better at controlling what they say to themselves and others about their performance during practice and competition. What you say to yourself and others affects your self-image, which limits your performance. Try this mental drill.

Purpose

This drill should help you avoid negative imprinting in competitions.

How to Do It

1. Set an objective at the start of a training day to run this drill a fixed number of times. If you are shooting X number of ends, try doing the drill every time today.

2. Shoot an end using your competition-grade mental process and shot routine.

3. Then, imagine you are asked by a competitor or training partner to comment on your performance.

4. When your shots were good, rehearse by saying, "I liked the way I (fill in with things you did well)." When things need improvement, rehearse by saying, "I need to remember to (state the correction needed)."

Tips

Your self-image imprints best immediately after the task ends. Controlling the first conversation you have with yourself and others is essential.

8.9 FUN VISUALIZATION

Purpose

This drill can convince you that visualizations have power.

Signs It Is Needed

If you struggle visualizing perfect shots when you are shooting (just before bow raise), you may need convincing or practice.

How to Do It

This is best done seated at a table. You will need a small weight, such as a metal nut, tied onto a piece of string. While resting your elbow on a table, hold the string so the nut is dangling. Try to make the string hang straight. Then visualize the nut making a circle about the size of a dime, clockwise. Don't try to manipulate the string—just visualize the movement and will it to happen. (Be fierce mentally!) It will happen. Then do the same for quarter-sized revolutions counterclockwise.

Tips

This is not magic! The muscle movements needed to make the motions happen are very tiny and best invoked subconsciously. The visualization constitutes instructions to your subconscious mind. (Like all good bosses, you are just describing what you want to happen and letting your minions figure out how to do it.)

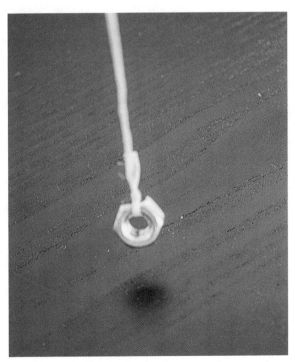

No, it is not magic; it is just a display of the power of your subconscious mind.

8.10 VERBAL CUING

Purpose

This drill teaches you how to reinforce a weaker shot element with verbal cues while shooting.

Signs It Is Needed

If part of your shot sequence breaks down under pressure, you need to learn how to fortify that element.

How to Do It

While taking shots, imagine that some part of your shot has weakened; your draw feels labored, your bow arm drops during the shot, or your followthrough is weak. While imagining one of these scenarios, devise a cue word or phrase you can use while performing that particular shot element. If your draw is weakening (e.g., through fatigue), mentally state the cue words "smooth and strong" while you are drawing. For a weak bow arm, it might be "strong bow arm," and for a weak followthrough, it might be "follow through" (slowly).

Tips

Cue words are for short-term use; do not get addicted to using them. They constitute small conscious reinforcements for largely subconscious processes.

Mentally: f-o-l-l-o-w t-h-r-o-u-g-h.

Purpose

Successful target archers limit their attention to what they are doing right now. This drill involves practicing just that.

Signs It Is Needed

If you shoot poor shots and afterward realize you were distracted, you need to practice shooting in "the now." Major breakdowns in an archer's shot often involve a breakdown in confining attention to the task at hand, moment by moment.

How to Do It

The first stage of this process is to make a list of all the things you need to attend to in order to make a successful shot. This list is far more extensive than a normal shot sequence. For example, the sequence step "nock an arrow" involves choosing an arrow to shoot, pulling it from your quiver, placing the nock at the nocking point (orienting the cock vane correctly), hearing the nock snap when pressed on (if snap nocks are used), correctly placing it on your arrow rest, and (recurve only) correctly placing it under the clicker.

Once you have your complete list, take shots while paying attention to each item on the list as you shoot. Move from item to item, with no breaks in concentration or attention. Do this for just a few shots.

Repeat as necessary.

Tips

This involves doing a task consciously rather than subconsciously, so it can be exhausting. When the task is done subconsciously, it feels almost effortless (it is not, it just feels that way). If you find your attention on something not on the list during the drill, modify the list.

8.12 STAYING PRESENT

Purpose

This drill focuses you on the present moment instead of the past or future. Thinking of events in the past or future results in poor shots.

Signs It Is Needed

You notice your thoughts drifting to the future (e.g., holding a trophy) or the past (e.g., that poor shot just before). Mentally replaying events that were less than desired is counterproductive. Staying present is the way your conscious thoughts guide your subconscious actions.

How to Do It

Start by focusing your breathing. Be aware of it. Actively try to bring your heart rate down by relaxing. It's okay for it to be escalated—it represents the thrill of the moment—but lower is better. Keep breathing steadily, evenly. Tell yourself you are going to really enjoy this shot—not the outcome, but the act of it. You are going to like it so much you wish to duplicate it. Smile the entire time you are thinking about your shot. If you drift into future thoughts, think about dinner plans, a soak in a hot tub, or a desired event that is unrelated to archery. When your thoughts shift to the task at hand, be thankful and happy to be there and enjoy each opportunity to the maximum. If you can do this, you have already succeeded.

After several minutes of staying present, take shots while being totally focused on your current shot. If you are distracted, or your thoughts move to the future or past, let down and start over. Commit to doing this, including letting down when your thoughts roam.

Variations

You can customize this drill to your abilities. The goal is to take control of your mind and steer it to work for you.

Tips

During practice, run through scenarios of importance that will raise your heart rate and escalate your emotional state. You will be teaching yourself that you can perform under these conditions, keeping fear out of the equation. Pretend you are in a one-arrow shoot off, closest to the middle wins.

MAKE IT A GAME

If you have a shooting partner, do a series of 10 one-arrow shoot-offs. In between each one, practice keeping yourself in the present, not thinking about the prize you will get for winning!

8.13 PLANNING IS A MENTAL SKILL

Purpose

This drill inculcates a habit of planning your participation in practice and competitions to better meet your goals.

Signs It Is Needed

If you find you cannot compete at a tournament because you are not a member of the sponsoring organization or you are inappropriately dressed to participate, or you cannot register for a competition because you did not compete in a qualifying event, you have failed to plan, which is the same as planning to fail.

How to Do It

Acquire either a notebook or a large annual calendar. This becomes your planning document. Start with your goals, maybe winning a state or regional tournament. There are any number of things required: having membership in the sponsoring organization (including having your membership card with you at the tourney), registering, paying entry fees, following dress codes, knowing shooting rules, making travel arrangements, arranging for lodging and meals . . . whew! Write all these things down as a checklist.

In addition, you may want to participate in preliminary competitions to prepare. If the goal is to participate in your first serious field tournament, you may want to schedule a preliminary field tournament so the important one is not your first. Also, there are implications for training. You may want to schedule a practice at a field range to get needed experience. So you will need to make practice plans.

Check your planning notes daily.

Tips

You can plan electronically, but electronic documents are easy to lose and hard to find once lost. (Out of sight, out of mind.) If you are adept at this, feel free to use your tools for this task.

Many archers use a larger notebook to record all the other things needed as well as their planning notes.

Many archers plan a season (indoor, outdoor) at a time.

8.14 KEEPING RECORDS IS A MENTAL SKILL

Purpose

This drill inculcates a habit of keeping records of scores shot in practice and competitions as well as other metrics that indicate progress.

Signs It Is Needed

Every serious archer needs to keep records. There are too many details to remember, and if you try you will forget important things. Keeping records allows you to track your progress to see whether you are improving. If not, you need to change what you are doing.

How to Do It

Acquire a notebook. This becomes your place to record important things. Start by recording practice round scores and competition round scores. Note the environmental conditions associated with each round. A graph showing a dip in performance a few weeks before makes sense when your notes point to rain and hail during the round!

Another thing to keep careful records of is your equipment. Knowing who made your last bowstring, how many strands were in it, what fiber was used, how long it was, how many twists were in it, and so on, becomes vitally important if you need to replace that bowstring. Note every change you make to your equipment. If you forget you made a change and your bow seems "off" somehow, you have no way of returning it to a formerly good state. Think of your notes as you would a computer backup. You may not need one all the time, but when you do, you really, really need one.

Make updating your records a habit.

Tips

You can keep records electronically, but electronic documents are easy to lose and hard to find once lost. (Out of sight, out of mind.) If you are adept at this, feel free to use your tools for this task.

Many archers use a larger notebook to record all the other things needed as well as their progress metrics notes.

Making graphs of scores in practice and competition is an easy way to see trends and determine the relationship between practice and competition scores. (For some archers, the practice scores are higher; for others the competition ones are.)

8.15 RELIEVING ANXIETY THROUGH PREPARATION

Purpose

This drill minimizes any anxiety you might experience during a competition by preparing for eventualities in advance.

Signs It Is Needed

If you experience panic during a competition anytime something goes wrong (e.g., equipment failure, rain), you need this drill.

How to Do It

At least a few weeks before a competition, sit down with a notepad and make a list of all the things that could go wrong during the competition. Such things include changes in weather (rain, wind), swarming insects, no food or water being served at the venue, first aid being needed, equipment failures, opponents cheating, and disqualifications because of rule violations. Go to extremes if you need to, but try to think ahead to every possible thing that could go wrong.

Consider solutions for each possible scenario:

- In case of rain, pack rain gear to wear (even practice in it if you haven't shot in it before).
- In case of small bites or scrapes, pack a first aid kit.
- For equipment failures, pack a spare tab, release aid, or bowstring (shot in and tuned), all the way up to a backup bow with all the accessories.
- Pack some energy bars in case there is no food served or you do not like the food served.
- Pack insect repellant, sunscreen, and so on.

If something occurs that you couldn't prepare for, you will have the peace of mind of knowing there was nothing you could have done beforehand. If something occurs that you did prepare for, then you are ready and your shooting will be minimally affected.

Tips

Reviewing this list before the competition can't hurt.

8.16 SCHEDULING MENTAL DRILLS DURING ARCHERY PRACTICE

Purpose

Mental skills, like physical skills, need to be practiced until they are second nature. Planning your practices helps ensure that you do some mental work alongside the physical work in your training sessions.

Signs It Is Needed

If you are stuck during a competition and you have a vague memory that there is a mental skills tool that could get you unstuck, but you can't remember it, you need this drill.

How to Do It

Practice plans do not need to be elaborate or fancy—they can be "back of an envelope" style—but in best record keeping practice, writing them down in your archery notebook is a good idea. The key is that each practice plan needs a segment that addresses mental skills.

Some mental skills need no planning. Once you have committed to making a pre-shot visualization of a successful shot, you do that every shot you make: practice or competition. But special tools don't get used as a matter of course. Here are some examples:

- *Fake a yawn.* When feeling pressure, fake a really big yawn and it will diminish.

- *Imagine shooting at home.* When feeling pressure, imagine you are shooting at your home range.

- *Imagine aiming dots.* When aiming off, it helps to imagine a contrasting color dot on your target face where you need to aim.

There are many more such mental tools, and each needs practice. Make a list of some of these to practice at each training session.

Example: To practice imagining aiming dots, deliberately mis-set your sight so your arrows are landing a hand's length high (or low, or left, or right). To get your arrows to land in the target center, you will need to aim off, and you can therefore practice imagining a brightly colored stick-on dot at the spot on the target where you need to aim.

After several shots aiming off, mis-set your sight in another direction.

Tips

Make a list of all the mental tools you find useful, and devise drills that will help you learn, and therefore remember, those tools.

Chapter 9

Competition Pressure and Ailments

As children, we often entered into competition with our peers. Having such a history, you would think we would all be experts at dealing with anything that comes up at competitions. Well, simply, we are not.

Archers experience all kinds of psychological heebie-jeebies when they are close to winning or in a shoot-off to determine a winner. We find ourselves shaking, sweating, talking and moving very quickly, and making mistakes we haven't made in years, and lots, lots more.

Sure, experience will cure all those ills, but those ills can also be responsible for preventing you from getting into those pressure situations in the first place. You can shake, sweat, and talk yourself right off the winner's podium.

You can prepare to deal with competition pressure. The key point is that everyone feels it. Some of sport's greatest athletes eagerly seek out the feelings associated with such pressure because those feelings tell them they are in the hunt. This is turning something one might characterize as bad into a very good thing, a thing to be sought and cherished.

These drills will give you a start on learning to deal with competition pressure.

One of the worst effects that can arise from competition is target panic. Target panic is the bane of a target archer's existence. And almost every serious archer gets it in some way, shape, or form.

Target panic has other names (e.g., gold shyness, buck fever, the yips), but it is a series of mental afflictions that can reduce even very accomplished archers to fumbling neophytes almost overnight. It is such a bugaboo that some archers will not even say the words *target panic* out of fear they will get it.

Target panic has a number of forms. One is freezing, the tendency for the archer's sight or arrow point to freeze on a spot on the target, and not a good spot either; or it can freeze on the correct spot but the archer can't get the shot off. Another form doesn't allow the archer's sight aperture to get anywhere near the target. Yet another is shooting spasmodically and in an uncontrolled fashion.

Target panic is thought to be responsible for more archers leaving the sport than all other causes combined.

But it is important that you know three things:

1. The symptoms are recognizable.
2. There is a "cure." (*Cure* is probably the wrong word, but it conveys the idea.)
3. You will probably need help.

Whole books have been written on the topic, so these drills are here to help with the greater process and are not a cure in themselves.

Archery is a fairly sedate sport, but injuries still happen. For serious archers, the more common serious injuries involve repetitive stress injuries of the joints in the arms, hands, and shoulders. For recreational archers, the most common injury is hitting one's arm with a bowstring.

It is very important to not ignore injuries to the fingers, wrists, elbows, and shoulders. Blithely assuming that things will get better is not the way to go. The most common sources of such injuries are shooting too much, shooting too much when training has been insufficient (especially shooting in competition, where one's focus is on scoring), and flawed form or execution (using the wrong muscles or skeletal structures). If these injuries were caused by archery in the first place, then the uncorrected causes will just continue to exacerbate the problems.

Always seek medical advice. If needed, take your bow with you to a consultation, and explain what it is you are doing so the medical professional can give you targeted feedback. If rehabilitation is recommended, fully rehab your injuries before resuming practice.

When you resume training, always start with very low-strain exercises: first a stretch band or tube, then a lighter drawing bow before picking up your normal bow. Share any relapses with your medical advisor. Pain, especially in the injured joints, must never be ignored. Soreness, to some extent, is expected when resuming archery activities, but if the soreness continues for days, consult your medical advisor.

All that being said, a few drills can help you work through your recovery successfully and even help prevent additional injuries.

There Is a Process: Curing Target Panic

Many archers have survived their encounter with target panic. You can, too. The process involved requires a great deal of dedication, time, and effort. There are no shortcuts. The amount of time required depends on the intensity of the symptoms. Note also that it's of benefit to have an experienced coach to help or at the minimum another archer who has experienced the process.

Some experts claim that if a person afflicted with target panic understands the symptoms and the causes of the panic, then the cure is easier to effect. We can't tell you that this is true or not. We suspect it is for certain types of people, but not for others. Plus the causes aren't necessarily known (they have something to do with anxiety).

Step 1: Fix Your Equipment Setup

If you are overbowed, using a release aid with a hair trigger, and have added lots of extra weight to your bow, any of these alone could prevent a successful treatment.

It is best to get equipment issues out of the way first, if for no other reason than it will lend confidence to the afflicted archer that the equipment is no longer a source of the problem. A good coach can really help here.

It also makes no sense to reprogram an archer's shot on a bow they will not be shooting later. A bow with a different draw length or different draw weight is, in effect, a different bow. We are so used to the adjustability of modern bows that we forget that if you wanted to move up five pounds in draw weight in the era of longbows and one-piece recurves, you had to acquire a different bow. We think that when we adjust our modern bows we have the same bow tweaked, but in fact, a different enough setup constitutes a different bow. Why try to retrain an archer to use a bow that is going to be changed significantly later? It makes no sense, so make equipment changes first.

Our opinion is that if someone is retraining to do a task, having different equipment makes it feel more like training to do a new task than relearning an old task, and we think that is all to the good. Training to do something only very slightly differently from what you have been doing is, we think, a tougher task, so making the bow feel quite different (if this is necessary) should help with the retraining.

Step 2: Fix Your Form

If you are leaning back while shooting, have your draw elbow much too low, or are punching your release aid, any of these could inhibit progress or even prevent a successful treatment.

If your draw length isn't right, the odds are you can't hold steady at full draw. If your draw weight isn't right, the odds are also that you can't hold steady at

(continued)

full draw. These are equipment issues, but the key thing is the holding steady. If the equipment issues have been fixed and your form still corresponds to the old setup, you are not going to hold well. A sight aperture or arrow point wavering all over a target face is not conducive to the calm state you want to create during a shot.

If you have no suitable coach nearby, consider recording yourself and seeing if you can get coached remotely; several very good coaches do this now.

Step 3: Fix Your Shot Sequence

So many archers have not written down their shot sequence. If you do have a sequence, you may have steps out of order, or you may be missing steps or have other issues that need to be addressed. Again, a good coach can help you with this.

The key aspect of using a shot sequence is the conscious control of what you want to be a subconscious process. You may already know you are capable of doing a great many things at the same time if they are subconscious, but only one thing at a time if thinking consciously (at most, two).

A great deal of work goes into drilling a process until it become subconsciously controlled. Examples are learning to tie your own shoes (or a necktie) and learning to drive a car. When you first attempt these tasks, it's like trying to herd cats. But after a few thousand repetitions, you can primarily do them on autopilot. We don't say "automatic" because that means you don't need to pay attention. Even though you are an expert at tying shoelaces at this point, you probably still make a mistake from time to time and need to retie a shoe. Think about it: What did you do when you retied those laces? Did you do a conscious "Step 1, cross the laces. Step 2, tuck . . ." process, or did you just somehow focus a bit more on the task? (*Hint:* It was the latter.)

This is what a shot sequence does for you. It moves your focus from one point to another through the process of executing a good shot. The shot occurs subconsciously, but the conscious mind is making sure the correct subconscious routine is running. It would be a disaster if "drive the car" all of a sudden showed up in the middle of a shot, now wouldn't it? This is basically what can happen to an archer without a drilled-in shot sequence.

The shot sequence, when identified and programmed consciously, herds the subconscious mind through the various subconscious subroutines involved in making a shot. It also gives the conscious mind something to do so it doesn't intrude on the process. When you are learning to drive, you are operating consciously: You are nervous and sweating; you don't know what to do or when to do it; you don't know what the lights mean in your dashboard display. When you have learned to drive, subconsciously you are relaxed and calm; you know what to do and when. Only if there is something way out of the ordinary (e.g., flashing red lights in your rearview mirror) does your conscious mind intrude.

Step 4: Create a New Shot Without a Target

If there is no target, there is no target panic, so it seems obvious that an archer should learn a reprogrammed new shot while shooting with no target face visible. Since there is no target, there is no advantage to shooting at distance, so the primary training tool is the blank bale (or empty bale) set up at minimum distance (three paces or so).

There are various guesstimates of how long this typically takes, from 21 days to three months. (The assumption is that training occurs on each day, so if you aren't training every day, adjust these estimates accordingly.) It is impossible to tell ahead of time how many days it will take. The only sure thing is that it will take as long it takes. Archers generally want to go fast; coaches want to go slow.

Since you can't predict for certain when this phase is complete, there at least need to be some indicators that suggest it is. Shooting an entire session blank or blind (eyes closed) bale while your coach or shooting partner is watching, looking for the target panic symptoms you were exhibiting and finding none, has to be one. Shooting a whole session of blank bale while executing properly is another. The worst-case scenario is to have you rush to shooting normally, only to have the symptoms come back. This is basically a waste of all the time spent in step 4 and a major setback. In itself, this establishes a need for some kind of test or bridge program between grinding blank bale practice and shooting normally.

Step 5: Incorporate a Bridge Program

Since the target is the primary focus for target panic, it needs to be reintroduced in such a way as to dilute its influence at the beginning and slowly reaccustom the archer to working with a target.

Bridge programs slowly introduce the influence of the target while the archer experiences high volumes of shooting success. There are a great many variations, but each incorporates these two points.

Look to the remaining drills in this chapter for examples.

9.1 THE FAKE YAWN

Purpose

This drill reduces the feeling of competition pressure.

Signs It Is Needed

If you find that being close to winning changes your behavior, you may be succumbing to competition pressure. This may take the form of shaking at full draw, shooting more slowly or rapidly, or many other forms.

How to Do It

You know how to yawn. Doing just that when you feel or anticipate competition pressure lessens the effects of the pressure (by simulating boredom, which is associated with yawns).

Variations

Yawns can be short or broad and long. Try various yawns to find the one that works best for you. Or use a big one when the pressure is big and a small one when you feel anxiety coming on.

Tips

This has to be practiced to make sure you can recall to do it when it is needed. You need to know what the signs of competition pressure are for you.

9.2 DISASTER RECOVERY

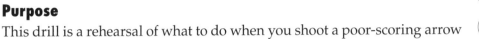

Purpose

This drill is a rehearsal of what to do when you shoot a poor-scoring arrow in competition but you do not know why.

Signs It Is Needed

All archers make poor shots for no obvious reason. This drill provides a routine for what to do after such shots.

How to Do It

Shoot your first arrow at 85 to 90 percent of normal tempo, with heightened focus on shooting correctly. If that shot is successful, the goal for the next two to four shots is to get up to normal shooting tempo. This drill is best done first when you begin shooting arrows in both practice and competition. Under the guise of a shooting warm-up, this makes sure your recovery routine is practiced and fresh.

Variations

When done as a shooting warm-up, start with one or two letdowns; this will provide a wake-up call for the muscles involved in shooting as well as a rehearsal for doing a letdown, should that be needed.

Tips

If your first recovery arrow ends up being shot as poorly as the one that prompted this routine, there is something else wrong and you must take additional measures to find it.

9.3 SIMULATING ANXIETY AND AROUSAL IN PRACTICE

Purpose

This drill simulates some of the effects of pressure you will feel in competition so as to acquaint you with them and teach you how to compensate for them.

Signs It Is Needed

Competition pressure may take the form of shaking at full draw, shooting slowly or rapidly, an elevated heart rate or breathing rate, and many other forms.

How to Do It

To simulate the arousal and associated elevated heart rate or breathing rate that can be caused by competition pressure, perform vigorous exercise for several minutes near the shooting line. This may involve vigorously running in place or doing jumping jacks or push-ups or other exercises that stress your arm and shoulder muscles. Then step to the shooting line with your bow and shoot under these conditions.

Tips

Take notes as to what effects you feel and how your shots were affected. Are your groups larger? Shifted left, right, up, or down? If there is a recognizable pattern, you may be able to compensate for the effects when they occur. Often, when you experience such things, the effects become smaller to the point that they are not even something to compensate for.

As you gain experience, note whether the effects of body arousal diminish. What is true for physical arousal is also true for mental arousal (anxiety), the effects of which should lessen with experience.

9.4 THE ONE-SHOT DRILL

Purpose

This drill simulates the feeling of an all-or-nothing shot such as can occur in one-arrow shoot-offs.

Signs It Is Needed

If the idea of a one arrow, closest-to-the-center shoot-off creates anxiety or physical symptoms of competition pressure (e.g., rapid breathing, rapid movements), you need to defuse this situation.

How to Do It

Before a practice session or at home or just before you put your bow away, take one shot (for all the marbles, Olympic gold, the world championship, whatever puts pressure on you).

Variations

People have been known to go to their range, unpack and set up, take their one shot, then pack up and go home.

Tips

The more you can visualize yourself in the scenario, the more effective the drill.

> ### MAKE IT A GAME
>
> If you have a shooting partner, you can hold a shoot-off. The higher-scoring arrow wins. (You decide on the prize ahead of time, possibly something like having to refer to the winner as "champion archer of the year" until the next shoot-off.)

9.5 A TIME-PRESSURE DRILL

Purpose

This drill simulates the time pressure you can feel in a timed end.

Signs It Is Needed

If you are nervous about shooting under the clock, this drill can make the situation more normal.

How to Do It

You will need a helper to count down the clock for you on a final, very important shot: 20, 19 . . . 3, 2, 1. Your job is to get an arrow out of your quiver and a shot off in good order before zero.

Variations

Start with 20 seconds per shot (a normal time allotted). Then reduce the time to 15 seconds, then 10, then anything under 10 that still lets you get away a shot in good order. It does you no good to try for times you cannot reach because this would be practicing distorting your own form. You want to know how many seconds it takes to get off a good shot.

Tips

The more you can visualize yourself in the scenario, the more effective the drill.

> ### MAKE IT A GAME
>
> If your helper is a shooting partner, you can do ends of three shots as a contest, with the one with the higher score the winner.

9.6 TARGET PANIC: RECOGNIZE THE SYMPTOMS

Purpose

This drill acquaints archers with the symptoms of target panic, which are observable all around if you know what to look for.

Signs It Is Needed

All archers need this information. Target panic is common and can be observed.

How to Do It

When observing any competition in person, on video, or on the Internet, take note of the symptoms you can see. Here is what to look for:

- *Flinching.* A rapid shudder going through the archer as if they were going to shoot but stopped themselves.
- *Snap shooting.* The archer releases shots the instant anchor is achieved or even earlier.
- *Freezing.* The archer is at full draw but can't release the bowstring.
- *Widely varying tempo.* Some shots are very slow; others are very quick.
- *Punching a release aid.* Compound archers can be seen jerking on the triggers of their release aids.

Even champions can be seen exhibiting these symptoms—even while winning (although this is rare)!

Tips

Some evidence is hard to see. At a recent Olympic Games, an archer had a teammate counting down the seconds on each shot while he forced himself to get shots off in the time allowed. The reason? Target panic.

Some time ago, one of the highest-ranked Olympic recurve archers in the world shot with a finger tab on top of a shooting glove. The reason? Target panic (he was trying to reduce the feeling in his fingers so his subconscious mind had less control and his conscious mind had more).

Important: The takeaway is not that you are doomed but that target panic is common, which means many people deal with it and overcome it. You can too! See the There Is a Process box.

9.7 TARGET PANIC: BRIDGING

Purpose

In getting back from target panic, it is not unusual to have to learn a different style of shot (some archers even switch from right-handed to left-handed shooting or vice versa). Once you have a shot in hand, you need to get back to being able to shoot targets comfortably. Programs that help with this are called bridging programs.

Signs It Is Needed

You are addressing your target panic and need to address shooting targets again.

How to Do It

This is a shooting drill, typically done indoors. Start with the largest target face available to you at a very short distance (five paces). Shoot five six-arrow ends for a total of 30 arrows. You must shoot five perfect scores. If you miss the center scoring ring in any of the rounds, you must start that round over.

After you've shot five perfect scores, move the target face five more paces away. Repeat the shooting process. Move the target face five paces farther away each time you register five perfect scores. When you reach 20 yards (18 m) (three sets of five rounds) and complete the task, move back to five paces and switch to the next smaller-sized target face (if you started with a 122-centimeter face, then 80 centimeters is next).

Repeat until you end up at the full distance with the regulation target face.

Variations

This drill depends greatly on your ability. If you are a highly accurate compound archer, you may want to use the X-ring as a "perfect" shot. If you are a weaker archer, you may want to use the 9-ring. Use whatever ring constitutes an excellent shot for you at this time.

To make the process more difficult, you can force yourself to restart the entire set of five scores (rather than just the round you are shooting) whenever there is a miss. To make it even more difficult, any miss takes you back to the five-pace distance. For massive difficulty, a miss takes you back to five paces and the largest target face.

Tips

It is very easy to lose focus and miss because the targets are so large and so close. Pay attention to what happens with your misses. The key to getting through this drill is focus and relaxation.

9.8 TARGET PANIC: BIG TARGET, LITTLE TARGET

Purpose

In getting back from target panic, it is common to begin shooting at big targets up close and bridge back to shooting smaller targets farther away, but some archers experience difficulties with that. This drill helps when making those transitions.

Signs It Is Needed

You are addressing your target panic and need to address shooting targets again but are having problems shooting anything but a very large target up close.

How to Do It

This drill is typically done indoors. Start with the largest target face available to you at a very short distance (five paces). Shoot at this target until you are comfortable. Then post the next smaller-sized target directly underneath the larger target.

Again shoot arrows at the larger target face, noting that you are comfortable doing that. Then switch to shooting at the smaller face. If you feel target panic symptoms coming back, switch to shooting at the larger face. When comfortable, switch back to the smaller target face.

Then move back from the butt a few paces and repeat.

When you achieve comfort with the smaller target face, swap the bigger face for the smaller and add the next smaller size below it; repeat the whole process.

After completing the drill indoors, you may need to repeat a similar process outdoors.

Tips

This will take quite a long time and require you to shoot many arrows. Focus on how it feels when you shoot. If you feel symptoms coming back, return to the higher target face and shoot until the symptoms are gone, then switch to the lower face. Repeat this over and over at different distances.

If you don't have room on your butt for the largest target faces, fold the edges back, exposing just the inner rings to make them smaller.

9.9 RETURNING FROM DRAWING SHOULDER INJURY

Purpose

This drill emphasizes keeping your draw arm low in the shoulder joint. This position provides reduced inflammation and additional clearance. Impingement can occur during shooting when the end of the humerus is too high in the shoulder joint.

First rehab and physical therapy are needed to recover from the injury. Once injury rehab is completed and shooting resumes, this drill teaches you to keep your shoulders low to prevent future damage. Even better, do this to prevent injury in the first place.

Signs It Is Needed

You develop pain in your drawing shoulder or have had a shoulder injury in the past.

How to Do It

Face a mirror with your complete archery rig. Emphasize dropping your shoulders as low as you can. Stand there relaxing your shoulders, watching them drop. As you raise your bow to draw, watch the movement of your shoulders in the mirror, and raise and draw your bow without raising either the front or rear shoulder—raise just your arms. Keep both shoulders as low as you can. As you draw, keep your drawing hand and bow hand at the same level. Line them up with each other in the mirror. As you draw, draw to your chest, not to your face. Once at full leverage, the final move is to your anchor position on your face. Practice doing this often (daily if possible) to teach yourself to keep your shoulders low. The value of this drill is many years of pain-free archery enjoyment.

Tips

Practice raising your arms while not raising your shoulders without your bow in your hand, using a mirror to monitor the movement. If you can do it without your bow, you will be able to duplicate it with your bow. It is natural to raise the shoulders when raising your arms. To learn not to is a tremendous advantage.

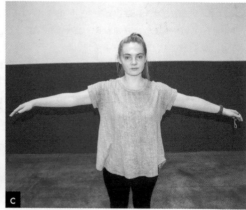

Suggested Resources

Ericsson, Anders. *Peak: Secrets From the New Science of Expertise*. Eamon Dolan/ Houghton Mifflin Harcourt, 2016.

Ferguson, Byron. *Become the Arrow*. Target Communications, 1994.

Kalym, Ashley. *Archery Fitness: Physical Training for the Modern Archer*. CreateSpace, 2015.

Kraemer, William J., and Fleck, Steven J. *Strength Training for Young Athletes*. 2nd ed. Champaign, IL: Human Kinetics, 2013.

Needham, Simon S. *Archery: The Art of Repetition*. Crowood Press, 2006.

USA Archery. *Archery*. Champaign, IL: Human Kinetics, 2012.

Wise, Larry. *Core Archery: Shooting with Proper Back Tension*. Target Communications, 2004.

About the Authors

Steve Ruis was the coach of the University of Chicago archery team (2011-2018) and has worked with a full range of students, from beginners to Olympic hopefuls, in the Chicago area. He supports two Junior Olympic Archery Development (JOAD) programs, is a member of two archery clubs, is a United States Collegiate Archery Association (USCA) certified judge, and still competes from time to time. He also has served as secretary of the Illinois Target Archery Association. He is a former USAA level 4 coach and NFAA master coach.

Courtesy of Steve Ruis

Ruis has been the editor of *Archery Focus* magazine since 1999 and has written 13 books on archery and coaching archery (including *Precision Archery*). He has written for *Archery* magazine of Japan and for *Bogensport Magazine* in Germany.

Mike Gerard is the owner of Jurassic Archery and has developed a number of archery-related products. He teaches both unlimited compound and release and Olympic-style recurve. He has trained a number of Junior Olympic Archery Development (JOAD) Olympians and Junior World Team members as well as adults.

Gerard was the National Intercollegiate Overall Champion in 1979 and the runner-up in 1980. He was winner of the U.S. National Indoor Championships in 1975 and again in 2015. He is a seven-time Huntsman World Senior Games champion (2011-2018). He is a member of USA

Courtesy of Mike Gerard

Archery and has served on the National Coaches Development Committee and the Board of Justice for USA Archery. Gerard has written articles for several archery magazines and has given numerous seminars on archery.